A HISTORICAL READER

World *War II*

nextext

Printed in the United States of America
ISBN 0-395-98666-4

1 2 3 4 5 6 7 8 9 0 — QKT — 06 05 04 03 02 01 00

Table of Contents

POETRY OF THE WAR:

PART II: WAR IN EUROPE AND AFRICA

PART IV: WAR ENDS

Vocabulary words appear in boldface type and are footnoted. Specialized or technical words and phrases appear in lightface type and are footnoted.

The Early Years

An American Reporter in Berlin

BY WILLIAM SHIRER

By late 1937, Hitler had been in power in Germany for more than four years. He had rebuilt the German military, begun a program of oppression of Jews, and had formed the Axis alliance with Italy and Japan. German troops had already positioned themselves menacingly on their borders. American journalist William Shirer was on assignment covering events in Europe. In his diary entry for September 27, he looks at the shadow of the Nazi movement and the dark, brooding cloud it brings with it.

BERLIN, September 27

Tess [Shirer's wife] back, feeling fine, and we're packing. We are to make our headquarters in Vienna, a neutral and central spot for me to work from. Most of our old friends have left . . . but it is always that way in this game. Go to London next week, then Paris, Geneva, and Rome to meet the radio people, renew contacts with the newspaper offices, and, in Rome, to find out if the Pope is really dying, as reported. We are glad to be leaving Berlin.

To sum up these three years: Personally, they have not been unhappy ones, though the shadow of Nazi fanaticism, sadism, persecution, regimentation, terror, brutality, suppression, militarism, and preparation for war has hung over all our lives, like a dark, brooding cloud that never clears. Often we have tried to segregate ourselves from it all. We have found three refuges: Ourselves and our books; the "foreign colony,"[1] small, limited, somewhat narrow, but *normal*, and containing our friends . . . ; thirdly, the lakes and woods around Berlin, where you could romp and play and sail and swim, forgetting so much. The theater has remained good when it has stuck to the classics or pre-Nazi plays, and the opera and the Philharmonic Symphony Orchestra, despite the purging of the Jews . . . have given us the best music we've ever heard outside of New York and Vienna. Personally, too, there was the excitement of working here, the "Saturday surprises," the deeper story of this great land in evil ferment.

Somehow I feel that, despite our work as reporters, there is little understanding of the Third Reich,[2] what it is, what it is up to, where it is going, either at home or elsewhere abroad. It is a complex picture and it may be that we have given only a few strong, uncoordinated strokes of the brush, leaving the canvas as confusing and meaningless as an early Picasso. Certainly the British and the French do not understand Hitler's Germany. Perhaps, as the Nazis say, the Western democracies have become sick, decadent, and have reached that stage of decline which Spengler[3] predicted. But Spengler included Germany in the decline of the West, and indeed the Nazi reversion to the ancient, primitive,

---

[1] foreign colony—the community of Americans, English, and others who live and work in Berlin but are not German citizens.

[2] Third Reich—the German Empire under Nazi rule.

[3] Spengler—German philosopher Oswald Spengler (1880-1936) argued that civilizations, like people, grow old and decay.

Germanic myths is a sign of her **retrogression**,[4] as is her burning of books and suppression of liberty and learning.

But Germany is stronger than her enemies realize. True, it is a poor country in raw materials and agriculture; but it is making up for this poverty in aggressiveness of spirit, ruthless state planning, concentrated direction of effort, and the building up of a mighty military machine with which it can back up its aggressive spirit. True, too, that this past winter we have seen long lines of sullen people before the food shops, that there is a shortage of meat and butter and fruit and fats, that whipped cream is *verboten*,[5] that men's suits and women's dresses are increasingly being made out of wood pulp, gasoline out of coal, rubber out of coal and lime; that there is no gold coverage for the Reichsmark[6] or for anything else, not even for vital imports. Weaknesses, most of them, certainly, and in our dispatches we have advertised them.

It has been more difficult to point out the sources of strength; to tell of the feverish efforts to make Germany self-sufficient under the Four-Year Plan, which is no joke at all, but a deadly serious war plan; to explain that the majority of Germans, despite their dislike of much in Nazism, are behind Hitler and believe in him. It is not easy to put in words the dynamics of this movement, the hidden springs that are driving the Germans on, the ruthlessness of the long-term ideas of Hitler or even the complicated and revolutionary way in which the land is being mobilized for Total War (though Ludendorff[7] has written the primer for Total War).

Much of what is going on and will go on could be learned by the outside world from *Mein Kampf*, the Bible

---

[4] **retrogression**—deterioration, falling apart.

[5] *verboten*—the German word for "forbidden," or "not allowed."

[6] no gold coverage for the Reichsmark—the currency is not backed up by gold reserves and is thus worthless outside Germany.

[7] Ludendorff—a German general in World War I, Erich Ludendorff (1865–1937) advocated in his 1935 work *The Nation at War* engaging all the energies of the nation, moral and economic, in a "total war."

and Koran together of the Third Reich. But—amazingly —there is no decent translation of it in English or French, and Hitler will not allow one to be made, which is understandable, for it would shock many in the West. How many visiting butter-and-egg men have I told that the Nazi goal is domination! They laughed. But Hitler frankly admits it. He says in *Mein Kampf*: "A state which in an age of racial pollution devotes itself to cultivation of its best racial elements must some day become master of the earth. . . . We all sense that in a far future mankind may face problems which can be surmounted only by a supreme Master Race supported by the means and resources of the entire globe."

When the visiting firemen from London, Paris, and New York come, Hitler babbles only of peace. Wasn't he in the trenches of the last war? He knows what war is. Never will *he* condemn mankind to *that*. Peace? Read *Mein Kampf*, brothers. Read this: "Indeed, the pacifist-humane idea is perhaps quite good whenever the man of the highest standard has previously conquered and subjected the world to a degree that makes him the only master of the globe. . . . Therefore first fight and then one may see what can be done . . . . For oppressed countries will not be brought back into the bosom of a common Reich by means of fiery protests, but by a mighty sword. . . . One must be quite clear about the fact that the recovery of the lost regions will not come about through solemn appeals to the dear Lord or through pious hopes in a League of Nations, but only by force of arms. . . . We must take up an active policy and throw ourselves into a final and decisive fight with France. . . ."

France is to be **annihilated**,[8] says Hitler, and then the great drive to the eastward is to begin.

Peace, brothers? Do you know what the *Deutsche Wehr*, which speaks for the military in this country, remarked two years ago? "Every human and social

---

[8] **annihilated**—completely destroyed.

activity is justified only if it helps prepare for war. The new human being is completely possessed by the thought of war. He must not and cannot think of anything else."

And how will it be? Again the *Deutsche Wehr*; "Total war means the complete and final disappearance of the vanquished from the stage of history!"

This, according to Hitler, is Germany's road. The strain on the life of the people and on the economic structure of the state already is tremendous. Both may well crack. But the youth, led by the S.S.,[9] is fanatic. So are the middle-class *alte Kampfer*, the "old fighters" who brawled in the streets for Hitler in the early days and have now been awarded the good jobs, authority, power, money. The bankers and industrialists, not so enthusiastic now as when I arrived in Germany, go along. They must. It is either that or the concentration camp. The workers too. After all, six million of them have been re-employed and they too begin to see that Germany is going places, and they with it.

I leave Germany in this autumn of 1937 with the words of a Nazi marching song still dinning in my ears:

> *Today we own Germany,*
> *Tomorrow the whole world.*

---

[9] S.S.—*Schutzstaffel*, the security service of the Nazis.

QUESTIONS TO CONSIDER

1. What reasons does Shirer give for general lack of understanding about what is going on in Germany?

2. What makes Germany "stronger than her enemies realize"?

3. What point is Shirer making by quoting from *Mein Kampf*?

The German Blitzkrieg in Poland

BY JAN NOWAK

Hitler's first move was to take possession of much of Eastern Europe. In 1938, he took over Austria, the Sudeten-land, and Czechoslovakia. In March of 1939, he signed a treaty with Stalin that promised he would not interfere with the Soviet Union's actions against Finland, Latvia, Estonia, eastern Poland, and eastern Romania if the Soviet Union would not interfere with Germany's plans. Hitler's first action after the treaty was the blitzkrieg, or "lightning war" in Poland. In this selection, Jan Nowak, a Polish officer, tells of the attack.

In the train from Poznan to Warsaw there was an air of almost joyful excitement. I had time to spend one day in Warsaw to say goodbye to my mother, my grand-mother, my brother, and my dachshund Robak. All were in good spirits. We were not alone: Poland had two powerful allies, France and Great Britain. The enmity between Nazi Germany and Soviet Russia made it certain—or so it seemed—that our eastern neighbor would preserve at least a friendly **neutrality**[1] . . . [no one expected] a secret German-Russian pact to partition Poland, signed before the Nazi troops crossed the Polish border.

When I reported for duty in the small town of Dubno, on the Russian border, my Second Squadron of Horse Artillery had already left and was in its battle position on the opposite side of the country, facing the German frontier. The reserve soldiers were collected in the barracks. When I left early in the morning to have breakfast in the officers' **mess**[2] on Friday, September 1, 1939, I saw another officer running toward me. Waving his hands he shouted excitedly: "The war has started— the fighting started at 5 A.M.!"

None of us realized that at that moment we had crossed a line that would cut our lives in half and forever prevent us from returning to what had been before. The excitement at the thought that history was knocking at our door did not last long. Our military convoy, bombed continuously by the Luftwaffe,[3] took three days to reach the reserve center for horse artillery at Zamosc, 150 miles southeast of Warsaw. The old fortress and the barracks could accommodate only some seven hundred reservists from all over the country. The center had only two field guns, so there was no question of conducting military exercises or preparations for battle. Condemned to enforced idleness, we lived through the nightmare of the next few days as spectators. During air attacks panicky soldiers and civilians sought shelter in the old forts, where the ceilings were in danger of collapsing even had there been no bombing. There were some **casualties**[4] in our small group. We looked at the endless processing

---

[1] **neutrality**—not taking sides; refusal to take part in a war between other powers.

[2] **mess**—dining hall.

[3] Luftwaffe—the German air force.

[4] **casualties**—dead and injured persons.

of civilians and soldiers, at the government cars filled with dignitaries escaping from Warsaw, at the convoys of civil servants evacuating the capital. England and France had declared war on Germany but as yet had made no move. German troops attacked from the west, from Czechoslovakia in the south, and from East Prussia in the north. A glance at the map showed that the country's armies were surrounded on all fronts. The German **ascendancy**[5] was shattering. News of the occupation of large towns like Katowice, Poznan, Cracow, and Lodz, one after the other, stunned us. As in a nightmare, we lost all conception of time and I cannot now remember the date on which we heard that the Germans had crossed the Vistula and were nearing Zamosc from the west and the south. . . . At last came the decision to evacuate the reserve center to the east, on foot, of course, for there was no motor transport. All semblance of order disappeared as we marched along outside the city. The main road was filled with refugees in carts, on bicycles, or on foot. . . . It was obvious that in such chaos we would cease to exist as a unit.

Someone in the group of my closest friends, young G., put forward his own plan. His father's estate was a few miles distant. We could get a cart and some horses there, and move on the country lanes in the direction of the River Bug. If, as the command of the center maintained, there was an organized front line at the river, we could ask to be admitted to the first unit we encountered. And if this line proved to be only imaginary, we could turn toward the Hungarian or the Romanian border. Anything not to be taken captive without having fired a single shot. We did not devote much time to discussing this plan. The next morning, from the house of Mr. and Mrs. G., we started across the fields on a cart pulled by two of their best horses toward the nearest

---

[5] **ascendancy**—domination, decisive advantage.

bridge on the River Bug. We crossed to the other side near a little village called Uscilug.

The stories of attempts to organize some resistance on the line of the River Bug, the last natural obstacle before the frontier between Poland and Russia, were not completely false. On both sides of the river one could see **camouflaged**[6] nests of machine guns, and the houses along the river were manned by considerable numbers of soldiers. We reported to the first senior officer we met in Uscilug. As far as we could see, he was organizing an operational unit on his own account. His method was to stand on the bridge, stop all the armed units withdrawing to the east, and, as long as they had no precise destination or orders, to take them under his command and deploy them to various positions along the river.

"You will report to Captain Herdegen," he commanded after we reported to him. I took heart when I heard that name. Witold Herdegen, an old friend of mine, was an officer of the Horse Artillery. He explained the situation to us. He had six field guns and a full complement of gun crews at his disposal. The guns were placed along the river, with two in front of the church. The terrain was quite favorable for defense: the east bank of the river rose almost straight up, several yards above the plain west of the River Bug. From there one could see clearly a sizable tract of land spreading beyond the edge of the forest.

"We shan't be able to resist long," said Herdegen, "but firing straight ahead we might have some superiority. We can get as many soldiers and officers as we wish. We must post military police on the road and stop those who are retreating. What we lack are guns, equipment, and ammunition. I don't even have a decent pair of field glasses."

---

[6] **camouflaged**—hidden, covered to look like the surroundings.

. . . On September 15 at about 9 A.M. the German motorized columns appeared in the distance from several directions, as predicted. Herdegen was observing the perimeter through a pair of **antediluvian**[7] field glasses, grabbed from a forester in the crowd of refugees. Through them one could see troop carriers covered with dark tarpaulins and tractors drawing field guns. For the time being Uscilug was silent. Only when the head of the column was about half a mile away did our guns begin to fire. At the same time, the field telephone rang: fire straight ahead. Direct fire at one mile is no great art: almost every shell meets its target. The German vehicles scattered and came to a halt. Their troops dismounted and dispersed into the fields. The caissons[8] were driven off the road, the drivers tried to loop back in the fields, found that they could not move forward, and so moved back seeking cover. Two or three guns got stuck in the roadside ditches, and we immediately took aim at them. Exploding shells put them out of action one after the other.

After about ten minutes the German artillery began to fire. At this point they were firing air-burst **shrapnel**,[9] highly dangerous to personnel, as the shells exploded right above our heads. My modest military knowledge, acquired in cadet school, was enough to tell me that this would not last long. Our guns were well camouflaged and our ammunition protected in dugouts, but the flash of our direct fire betrayed our positions. As soon as their heavy artillery showed up, it would finish us off in a few minutes. For the moment, though, we tried to ignore the shrapnel and were hitting the German vehicles one after the other, though most of them were empty by now. One of our loaders got hit in the back,

---

[7] **antediluvian**—literally meaning "before the flood (in the Bible)," extremely old and out of date.

[8] caissons—horse-drawn ammunition vehicles.

[9] **shrapnel**—a shell filled with small metal balls that explodes before it lands.

but his place was at once taken by a cadet officer. After a while Herdegen came up and said: "Our gun on the other side of the Lug has been silent for three-quarters of an hour. They may have all been hit, or they may have run away. Take four men with you and go and find out what has happened. If they are all dead or wounded or have gone, get the gun back in action. There should be plenty of ammunition left. . . ."

Uscilug took its name from the mouth (*ujscie*) of the River Lug, which, at the southern end of the village, ran along a fairly deep gully to the Bug. Not far off, on the opposite high bank of the Lug, there was a row of peasant huts, and it was there that we had to go. We skirted the deserted village in a wide circle, as Herdegen had ordered, and halted on the fringe of a small grove of trees. A sizeable field of stubble still separated us from the huts behind which our gun should have been. At that moment one of the men called out in a panic: "Sir — Germans!" He was pointing to the left. About four hundred yards away, the road crossed a field sloping gently down to the river. I could not see anything. "Are you dreaming or what?" I shouted. "There are no Germans here." But others then said that they had seen a few helmets showing, so there must be a detachment there. I decided to wait a few minutes. I was beginning to be puzzled by the absence of any sound from the huts, a hundred steps in front of us. There should have been a considerable number of our troops there.

After a few minutes I decided to abandon caution. I drew my pistol from its holster and said firmly: "There aren't any Germans here. We shall cross the field at the double: follow me!" I emerged from cover certain that the other four would follow, but halfway across the field I saw that none of the soldiers had budged. At the same moment I heard the whine of a bullet, then a second and a third. I looked to the left and, far beyond the road, saw Germans rising to their feet. I ran toward the nearest hut, still many yards away. Bullets were hitting the dried-out soil all round me, sending puffs of dust into the air, but I reached the fence **unscathed**[10] and sprang over it (though I was no athlete). I found myself in the courtyard of a farm. I did not have a second to lose. Without hesitation I threw myself into a large pile of straw in a corner where the farmyard wall joined the hut. Hardly had I done so when Germans appeared in the courtyard. They didn't see me and ran off in pursuit of a soldier who had crossed the field outside a moment earlier. . . .

For a while everything was silent, but after fifteen minutes or so I heard German voices again. They returned to the courtyard, but this time not in pursuit.

I could not see anything, but from the feverish pitch of the commands being given I guessed that they were setting up a machine gun post only about a dozen steps away from where I lay. A few minutes later there was a long burst of fire. An immediate answer came from the other side of the Lug, so I knew that our men had not been taken by surprise.

I attempted to work out what had happened. While their artillery was bombarding Uscilug, the Germans must have built a **pontoon**[11] bridge a few miles south of the village in order to outflank us. Our men at Uscilug must have realized that a considerable force was advancing on them and decided to withdraw beyond the Lug, where they could better defend themselves. I assumed that, after an exchange of fire, the Germans would push on through the gorge to drive us out of Uscilug and secure the crossing of the River Bug. . . .

I began to consider the possibility of escape. If I waited until nightfall, I might manage to creep through the undergrowth and return to my position at Uscilug.

---

[10] **unscathed**—unhurt.
[11] **pontoon**—a floating structure.

I might also attempt to go further east. After a few hours the German voices became more distant, but, alas, toward dusk they were heard again. Apparently they intended to spend the night here, in the hut and in the barn. Escape would not be easy.

Dusk began to fall. Suddenly I heard heavy steps coming straight toward my hiding place. A German, almost touching me, pulled out an armful of straw and walked away. There was now not a second to lose: the Germans were collecting straw for bedding. If I tried to cross the courtyard, they would shoot me on sight. The only way out was over the farmyard wall. I recalled that in the morning a German who was pursuing me had jumped it and I was trying to remember how high it was. Suddenly that German was back reaching for more straw from the pile but his hands found me instead. He shouted with fright. Pushing him away with all my strength, I leaped out of the straw and tried to grab the top of the wall, but it was too high and I fell flat on my back. In a flash there were two Germans on top of me. Others rushed out of the hut and pinned my legs and arms to the ground, all shouting at once. I got a sharp kick in my side, which took my breath away. I was sure that in a moment they would either trample me to death or shoot me, but, having recovered from the shock of finding me, the Germans, or rather Austrians, as they turned out, dragged me to my feet and into the hut. They took away my revolver and emptied my pockets. To hell with the revolver, I thought, but I was sorry to lose my good old turnip-shaped Omega pocket watch, which had been my father's.

My captors looked at me with interest. My knowledge of German was very limited, but in the group there was a student from Vienna who spoke passable French. They fired questions at me. How did I get there? What was I up to? How long had I been there? In a short while, they brought me a canteen full of hot soup and a piece of rye bread. The Austrians are not like the Germans, I thought; they treat a prisoner like civilized people. To my delight, they returned to me not only my documents and my wallet, with the money still in it, but also my father's watch and my forage cap, which they had found in the straw.

An hour later, three armed soldiers escorted me to a **lorry**[12] waiting on the road. The night was bright with the glare of fires: Uscilug was burning, but no sounds of battle could be heard. We crossed the river on the pontoon bridge. The vehicles that we had shelled the previous day were there; several which had been destroyed had been dragged into a ditch. I was told to sit on the ground and not to move. I was wearing fatigues, and after the warm day, the September night was cool. The ground was covered with dew, and my teeth were chattering from the cold. The soldier guarding me noticed this and without a word threw me a blanket from the lorry.

It was almost light when a group of German soldiers came by and saw me. One of them stopped, pointed to my spurs, and, with a rough gesture, indicated that I was to give them to him. Slowly and reluctantly I loosened the leather straps.

"Schnell!" ("Quickly!") he roared.

I felt as if somebody had slapped my face. Only then did I realize the full indignity of being a prisoner. I felt as if my life were over. The state of Poland, whose resurrection I had observed with my own eyes and which had seemed a mighty **edifice**,[13] had collapsed like a house of cards in a few weeks. After only one day at the front I was a captive. I fell into a depressed and indifferent gloom, from which I was awakened by a strange commotion. The Germans, my guard included, started

---

[12] **lorry**—a long, flat, horse-drawn wagon without sides.
[13] **edifice**—large, impressive symbol.

shouting to one another and running into the fields. I remained all alone, sitting above a ditch beside a German lorry. I looked up and saw a formation of bombers approaching from the south. . . .

For so many days we scanned the cloudless September skies for at least one Polish bomber—and now here is one at last. Bombs will begin to drop now, I thought. Too late; I don't care whether I am hit or not. It doesn't matter now; I shan't bother to move. But suddenly a thought flashed through my mind: Why should I be killed by a Polish bomb? I slowly raised myself from the ground and had run only a few feet into the field when I heard the characteristic whistle behind me. I did not have time to throw myself down before a powerful blast picked me up and flung me about five yards away. There was a long series of explosions, then silence. I got up and looked back at the place where I had been sitting. There was a **crater**[14] two yards deep. Of my blanket only a few scattered scraps remained. A car was turned over on its side and crushed, as if someone had squashed it into the ground with a giant boot. I too would have been squashed into a bloody mess had instinct not saved me in that last second.

Around me I could hear moaning. Although the bombing had not been very accurate, some shrapnel had hit the lorries in which soldiers were sleeping. The survivors were pulling out the dead and wounded, and vehicles marked with a Red Cross began to arrive: also a jeep came and took me away.

On the journey a few other prisoners of war, officers and other ranks, were picked up. From them I heard that the Germans had withdrawn from Uscilug, which had been abandoned and burnt by our forces, to the opposite side of the Bug. Why didn't they push further east, I wondered, just as I had wondered the day before why we did not see a single German plane overhead.

---

[14] **crater**—a hole in the ground where a bomb has exploded.

On September 17 we were delivered to a large assembly point in a churchyard for all the prisoners from the area. The Germans had surrounded and disarmed several Polish divisions, and new groups of Polish troops were arriving all the time. Now we were no longer in the hands of the Austrians but of the Germans, who treated us brutally. A few officers of the Wehrmacht (or perhaps it was already the Gestapo[15]) began to select Jews "by sight." They avoided officers, but concentrated on privates and non-commissioned ranks, pulling out soldiers with "Semitic" features and leading them away, to the accompaniment of shouts and face-slapping. They tried to drag away an officer cadet, who answered them haughtily in German quoting the Geneva Convention. Deathly pale, he showed them an identity card on which his religion was shown as Roman Catholic, and also produced a religious medal from under his shirt. The Germans then let him go. We observed these scenes with clenched teeth and a feeling of helpless fury.

Late in the afternoon further groups of prisoners were brought in, bearing other news. That morning the Soviet troops had crossed the Polish frontier, advancing toward Lwow. At first this news was received with delight. Now we thought there would be a clash between Hitler and Soviet Russia. Everything might change. But the new arrivals soon dampened our joy. From communiqués[16] issued in Moscow and Berlin, it appeared that the Red Army had entered Poland by agreement with Hitler and that it was going to occupy the eastern part of the country. This explained why the Germans had withdrawn from Uscilug. The River Bug was to be the new Russo-German boundary line. A gloomy silence fell . . . .

---

[15] Gestapo—the state police under the Nazis, known for their terrorist methods.

[16] communiqués—official bulletins.

I turned around and saw a slim, handsome lieutenant with an oval face and regular features who had until then been silent. A few hours later I learned that his name was Jozef Cyrankiewicz, a well-known Social Democrat in Cracow who had been especially active in politics among the students of Jagellonian University.

The number of prisoners collected by the Germans was too great for their transport and supply facilities, the more so as bridges and railway lines were mostly destroyed. An enormous column of perhaps several thousand prisoners was formed and sent off on foot to the railway station of Jaroslaw, some seventy miles away. The railway line from Przemysl to Cracow was practically the only one still functioning. Our column was so long that from its head one could not see the rear. It was guarded by soldiers on lorries with machine guns pointed at the marching men and by guards on foot spread along both sides of the road. There was no possibility of escape. The Germans repeatedly warned that they would open fire upon anybody who left the road.

Before nightfall we were locked up in churches or farm buildings that were easy to guard. There was so little room that in the churches we slept mostly sitting up where we could: on the benches, on the stone floors, on the altar steps. Most comfortable were the **confessionals**.[17] Food was scarce. On the first day the Germans halted the column and allowed us to spread out within a radius of a hundred yards or so to dig potatoes. In the evening they brought cauldrons of soup. The next morning, before the march was resumed, they brought us coffee and loaves of bread. There was not enough food for everybody, and there were ugly scenes when it was distributed. One could then learn to what **degradation**[18] one can sink when one feels hungry or

---

[17] **confessionals**—small, enclosed stalls where priests hear confession.

[18] **degradation**—sink to a low state, usually accompanied by feelings of shame and worthlessness.

even fears that one might become hungry. People fought to be allowed to hold the soup kettles and the stacks of bread, and later fought again over the distribution of the food. Those who did not wish to engage in an undignified scramble after the day-long march went hungry.

The officers and officer-cadets whom the Germans put at the heads of columns to guard them better and to separate them from the other ranks were in a slightly better situation because in the villages peasants pushed into our hands whatever they had to give: an apple, some broad beans, a slice of bread, a single cigarette, glasses of water, a few baked potatoes. A little woman who had nothing else to give pushed a few **nasturtiums**[19] into my hand. The peasants had nothing left by the time the rear of the column reached them. The Germans did not interfere, on the whole. Lack of supplies also presented a problem for them.

There were ever more frequent cases of fainting from hunger and exhaustion, but the worst thing was to hear the constant complaints not only against those responsible for our defeat but against the whole nation. There was some kind of compulsion to heap abuse on one's own people. . . .

On Cyrankiewicz's initiative the first "conspiracy" was **concocted.**[20] We decided to use our influence to restore some morale, discipline, and dignity to our ranks and to react strongly against any slur on our nation, government, or army. We stood guard in turn during the distribution of food, each guard taking the last smallest portion. The food obtained from the peasants in the villages went into a common pool and was fairly shared. The results of these **endeavors**[21] were quickly evident. As soon as the "conspirators" gained

---

[19] **nasturtiums**—small, orange flowers.
[20] **concocted**—put together.
[21] **endeavors**—works.

confidence, a **modicum**[22] of order was restored, at least within the group nearest us. After two days' march we were loaded onto lorries and driven toward Jaroslaw.

There we were loaded into cattle trucks forming a train about a mile long. We noticed that our German escort was well armed, but numerically weak. When we stopped at a station, POW's under guard had to carry round buckets of water and bread. As the opening and shutting of wagon doors each time took a lot of time, they took to leaving the doors open. On the fifteenth wagon, machine guns were mounted on each side. We were warned many times that the guards were under orders to open fire if there were any attempt to escape.

During the night a thick fog descended and the train had to slow down to about twenty-five miles per hour. Someone suggested that we should try to escape then, because by first light we would be inside the borders of the Reich, and it would be too late. We were excited by the idea, but opinions were divided. Someone pointed out that we were in uniform and that we didn't know whether there were any German detachments in the area. Besides, the guards had enough machine guns to finish us all off even if they couldn't see well to aim in the dark.

"We must wait until we are nearer Cracow," said Cyrankiewicz. "I know a workers' settlement there not far from the railway lines. They will certainly hide us and give us civilian clothes."

A group was immediately formed of those who wanted to jump from the train. Cracow drew nearer. In the fog and darkness it was difficult to recognize our precise location.

---

[22] **modicum**—small amount.

"I think it's here," said Cyrankiewicz. "Let's go!"

We had already drawn lots to decide on the order in which we would jump. I was third. We had to jump one after the other, very quickly, to reduce the danger for those following. I jumped sideways and fell hard against the sloping embankment, rolled down it, got to my feet and started running blindly forward, sometimes tripping over bushes or tree roots. I must have run about a hundred yards when the machine guns began to fire. I looked quickly behind me. The train not only did not stop; it seemed to have speeded up, so there would be no pursuit. I started running again and heard the pounding feet and heavy breathing of my friends.

We reached some buildings. The inhabitants, awakened by the firing, were looking through the window-panes. I rushed into the first house, breathless, capable only of saying single words: "Germans . . . escaped . . . from train." I pointed back in the direction from which long bursts of machine gun fire were still audible. A very large old woman in a shift and bodice without a word pushed me into the bedroom, threw me into a still warm bed, and covered me with an enormous feather quilt. I felt suffocated and tried to move, but she weighed about one hundred eighty pounds. For several minutes I attempted to get my breath. I was covered by the quilt, the pillow, and the owner of the bed. Some interminable minutes later, she must have decided that the danger was over and the terrible weight shifted. I extricated myself and sat on the edge of the bed. In front of me, staring, was the whole family.

"Thank you," I gagged, taking a deep breath with great relief. I was free.

QUESTIONS TO CONSIDER

1. Why was there "almost joyful excitement" when Nowak was preparing to go to war?

2. What accounts for the very rapid success of the German attack?

3. How does Nowak's attitude about the war and his role in it change after the German soldier commands Nowak to hand over his spurs?

Jews in Hiding

BY ROSE SILBERBERG-SKIER

Hitler's war on the Jews of Europe began the year after he became chancellor of Germany. Beginning in 1933, a campaign of terror first stripped Jews of legal rights, attempted to drive them out of German-held lands, and encouraged hate crimes against them. Then, in the night of November 9, 1938, SS troops took to the streets, smashing the windows of Jewish businesses and destroying property. This night, the night of broken glass, or Kristallnacht, *signaled the beginning of the Holocaust, as Jewish citizens were rounded up and killed or sent to concentration camps. In parts of Europe, some Jews were able to survive by hiding in the homes and farms of non-Jewish people. The following is an account of Rose Silberberg-Skier, who survived the Holocaust in Poland.*

I come from an enormous family of Hasidic Jews who were very, very religious. Generations back, one of my relatives was a famous rabbi. Until the Germans invaded Poland, we all lived near my grandfather, an hour away from the city of Krakow. Every Saturday after synagogue the grandchildren would gather at his house and line up for a chocolate wrapped in fancy paper.

Both my father and my mother worked in my grandfather's printing business. While they were away, a maid took care of me. On Sundays, without anyone knowing, she took me to church with her. I'd chant the prayers and stare at the beautiful statues.

In 1939, when I was five and my sister Mala was an infant, the Germans invaded Poland. Word soon spread that they were shooting the Jewish men in the small towns and villages. My father said we should go to the city, where he thought it would be safer. When we returned to our town, we found that many of my uncles had been killed.

Meanwhile my grandfather, a widower, had left for Palestine hoping to get homes for us there. By the time arrangements were made, the British, who governed Palestine, wouldn't let more Jews in. So my grandfather stayed there while we were stuck in Poland.

First the Germans forced us and thousands of other Jews into the Srodula Ghetto in one of the poorest Polish neighborhoods. They gave the Poles our beautiful homes and shoved us into tiny shacks. We were seventeen people in two rooms. The only way we could get food was by bribing the Germans with jewelry and other valuable possessions. Others, who weren't lucky enough to have anything to trade, died of starvation.

In the **ghetto**[1] the Germans kept announcing that parents should send their children to the Jewish-run school, but my parents decided to teach me reading and arithmetic at home. One day the Germans surrounded the school and took all the children away.

When my father realized how dangerous things were, he contacted a Polish woman he knew named Stanislawa Cicha and offered to pay her for hiding us in

---

[1] **ghetto**—walled-in sections of cities where Jews were centralized by Nazis.

the chicken coop connected to her house. Mrs. Cicha agreed, and my father quickly began to make the coop livable.

At this time you could still leave the ghetto before curfew, so my father worked on the coop in every spare moment. First he boarded up its only window so no one would see what he was doing. Then he furnished it with a small table, some chairs, and pads for us to sleep on. He also built a tiny **bunker**[2] under the floor for added safety and piled potatoes on top of the trap door to mask it. The bunker was windowless, with only enough air to breathe for a few hours, but in an emergency it would protect us.

Finally everything was ready, and the four of us and my Uncle Israel slipped out of the ghetto in the middle of the night. We began living in the cramped coop, which was dark and smelled from the chickens that Mrs. Cicha used to keep.

From the beginning we depended totally on Mrs. Cicha. She brought us our food and water and emptied the pail we used as a toilet. If the time ever came for us to hide in the bunker, she'd be the one who'd lift open the trap door to let us out.

Mrs. Cicha was originally from Lithuania and was married to a Polish man who was now in a labor camp in Germany. She had no children, no close friends, and no relatives living nearby. Except for her dog, Rex, and the rabbits, turtles, and cats she kept inside with her, she was alone.

But she had a neighbor in the house attached to hers. This woman, Mrs. Dudwalka, hated Jews. If she had known we were in the coop, she gladly would have turned us in. All day she sat at her window watching people go by, so we never went out.

---

[2] **bunker**—a place for people to hide, usually underground.

And we always had to be silent. Even walking on the wooden floor was dangerous, because the planks creaked and that noise might arouse Mrs. Dudwalka's suspicion. Besides, Mrs. Cicha was a seamstress, and her customers came to the house to have their clothes fixed. When they were around, we went barefoot or sat in one place for hours.

My sister by then was only two and a half and didn't understand why she couldn't run about or speak above a whisper. No matter how hard my parents tried to discourage her, Mala kept climbing up to the coop's tiny hayloft and singing in a loud voice. Finally, to protect all of us, my father asked a Polish family he knew if they could hide her. He told them that my Aunt Sara Wachsman, who was passing as a Christian, would bring them money each month.

This couple had two teenage sons and were delighted to have a little girl in the house, but they had to be careful. They said they were willing to take Mala if they could change her name to Mary and after the war convert her to Catholicism. They also wanted my father to promise that one day Mala could marry one of their sons. My Orthodox[3] father had a difficult time making a decision. In the end, he agreed.

By then food was scarce. Mrs. Cicha's coupons barely got enough for her, and with us to feed it was even harder. Sometimes she bought things on the black market, but that wasn't safe because people might notice her carrying home too much.

It hurt my father to see us go hungry. And he hated living in the coop. When Aunt Sara told him that the Germans were giving out food coupons to ghetto Jews who registered for identification papers, he said we should go back there.

---

[3] Orthodox—a branch of Judaism whose members closely follow the precepts of the Torah, including the eating of Kosher foods and observing the laws of the Sabbath.

My mother thought it was a bad idea but gave in. Finally the two of them and Uncle Israel left for a few days to see how things were. While they were gone, Aunt Sara stayed with me.

The ghetto had quieted down, so my parents stayed there. Usually Aunt Sara kept me company, but sometimes she too disappeared, and then I was alone in the coop. I was terrified. Every strange noise made me think someone was coming to get me.

At night, Mrs. Cicha brought me food, and I'd whisper to her how horrible I felt. She'd say, "Don't worry. Things will get better." But I didn't believe her.

To keep me busy, Mrs. Cicha gave me a pen and paper, and I wrote letters and drew pictures, which Aunt Sara delivered to my parents. I also read and reread the books my parents had left for me. A while back my mother had found an empty German cigarette carton that had swastikas on one side and was plain on the other. I cut the carton into a lot of pieces and made playing cards with them, drawing a chicken for the queen and a rooster for the king. But I was bored and lonely. I missed my mother.

Once my parents came to the coop for a short stay. I heard my mother press my father not to go back to the ghetto. She said it was getting more and more dangerous there and, also, she didn't like leaving me by myself. But my father wouldn't listen. Instead he suggested I come now and then to stay with them.

So at night, in the spring and summer of 1943, Aunt Sara would sneak me into the ghetto, and I'd spend a week or two with my parents. After being shut up in the tiny dark coop, the ghetto was a treat. There were other nine-year-olds to play with, and I could go outdoors.

One Sabbath in July when I wasn't scheduled to visit my parents, I begged Aunt Sara to take me anyhow so I could spend Shabbat[4] with them, and she did.

---

[4] Shabbat—the Sabbath, the holy day of the week, in which Jews worship, rest, and do not work.

The next morning when I awoke, the ghetto was surrounded by the SS with guns pointed in every window. On loudspeakers they said that all Jews were being sent to work camps and should go to the train station.

My father knew about a bunker that was entered through a stove, and we crawled in, one after another, with thirteen people following behind. But the SS dogs soon found us, and we had to come out.

By then the trains to the camps were filled, so we were told to wait in our room until the next day. Since Aunt Sara had Christian papers and fair hair and I was blue-eyed, my father thought we could pass as Gentiles[5] and might be able to escape. But with his heavy Yiddish[6] accent and he and my mother not having Aryan papers,[7] he felt they had no chance.

He told us about another bunker, which was above a chandelier and was stocked with food. We could hide there for a few days until things were safe. Then he made me recite the address of cousins in Jerusalem and said that after the war, I should find a way to get to them. "I will try to come too, but if not, they will take care of you. Your job is to remember you are Jewish."

The next morning my mother hugged me good-bye and promised me we'd see each other again. As she and my father walked in one direction, Aunt Sara and I went in the other. I looked back to see my mother's face once more, but only my father turned around for a moment.

There were sixteen of us crammed into the attic above the chandelier. It was very hot, and we had no water. Through a hole in the wall we could see the SS running around below, emptying the ghetto of thousands of Jews.

---

[5] Gentiles—to Jews, people who are not Jewish.

[6] Yiddish—the language spoken by most East European Jews prior to World War II.

[7] Aryan papers—identification papers that proved a person was of the "correct" race, according to the Nazis.

Suddenly one man in the bunker, who had watched his baby killed by the Nazis, decided to give himself up. No one could change his mind. When he lowered the chandelier to climb out, the SS saw him. In seconds they directed their machine guns at us. I was so petrified, I couldn't move or speak. I thought this was the end.

We were all taken to a hospital to wait there for a van that would take us to Auschwitz concentration camp, ten miles away. "Do you want to live?" Aunt Sara asked me. I shook my head yes. "Then you've got to escape," she said. She brought me to a window and pointed out the road to Mrs. Cicha's house.

But I had never traveled alone in the city, and I didn't know what Mrs. Cicha's house looked like in the daylight. I was scared.

Aunt Sara spoke to Mr. Feder, a Jewish man she knew in the hospital who was being forced by the Germans to work as a policeman. She offered him a diamond to let me out, but first he made her give him Mrs. Cicha's address so he and his wife could escape there too.

For the next five hours I crawled on my hands and knees through tall grass along a ravine, trying to keep out of sight of the SS. When I was about to cross the bridge leading to the Christian sector, some Polish teenagers who should not have been on the Jewish side started tormenting me with their dog. "It's a Jew! Its a Jew!" they shouted. "Let's call the SS." I thought, *Now* my life is over.

Suddenly out of nowhere a Polish woman appeared and yelled at the boys to leave me alone. She told me where to find the nearest streetcar and said I should get moving quickly. It was Sunday, and Aunt Sara had reminded me that Catholic children would be coming from church wearing clean clothes. She said I should pick some wildflowers and use them to hide my dirty face and dress. Hurriedly I did this.

When I finally got to Mrs. Cicha's door, I was trembling. She pulled me in and asked where the others were. Then she gave me water to wash myself and took me into the coop. My Uncle Sam Klapholz and Uncle Israel, who both had escaped from the ghetto, were there, but not my parents. I was afraid to think where they could be.

A few days later Mr. Feder came with his wife, and then Aunt Sara arrived with Aunt Bela. Right after that other Jews who knew Mrs. Cicha came too. There were sixteen of us in that little space.

Mrs. Cicha couldn't possibly feed us all. Once a week she brought some food that Aunt Sara cooked on a small stove, but the rest of the time we had only bread. The limit for each person was two slices a day. I cut mine into a hundred tiny pieces and every ten minutes ate a morsel to make it last longer.

Meanwhile my parents still had not come. I kept looking at a picture of my mother that I had with me and couldn't stop whimpering.

Then unexpectedly, in January 1944, the family who had been hiding Mala brought her to the house. They said they couldn't keep my sister anymore because their neighbors suspected she was Jewish and had threatened to call the Gestapo. Mala was now four and a half. As soon as she saw me, she rushed into my arms and whispered in my ear, "I can tell *you* that I'm Jewish."

This time I was determined not to let anyone take Mala away again. The minute she sneezed or coughed, I rushed to cover her mouth, petrified someone would hear her. If she climbed up to the tiny hayloft, I quickly grabbed her and told her to sit still.

Five weeks after Mala arrived, Aunt Bela got a letter from her husband, who was in a concentration camp. It was delivered by a Polish foreman who worked there and said that my uncle was alive. Aunt Bela wrote a note back in Yiddish and gave it to the foreman.

A few days later, in the middle of the night, there was loud banging on Mrs. Cicha's door. From the coop I heard SS men shouting, "Where's the Jewish woman?" They had stopped the Polish foreman to check his identification and found Aunt Bela's letter on him.

Within seconds Uncle Israel pushed open the boarded window of the coop and jumped out, while Uncle Sam threw me into the bunker. After he helped Aunt Sara and Aunt Bela down and piled up the potatoes, he closed the trap door and left through the window. Suddenly from above I heard Mala crying, "I want my sister." In the confusion my Uncle Israel, who was responsible for hiding Mala, had panicked and forgotten her.

The SS men came into the coop and grabbed Mala. It was winter, and Mala wasn't even wearing a coat or shoes. They also arrested seven of the others, who weren't able to get out in time. They took Mrs. Cicha, too. Then they boarded up the house.

For an hour Aunt Sara, Aunt Bela, and I waited in the bunker, wondering who'd come to lift open the trap door for us. We were so worried. Finally Uncle Sam let us out. He had taken a huge chance coming back to the house but said he could never forgive himself if he left us there.

He advised Aunt Sara and me to go to a Polish woman he knew to get false passports and new identity papers. The man who forged the papers wrote that we were Christian and that I was Aunt Sara's daughter. He suggested we go to Germany where they were hiring Polish women to work and Aunt Sara could pass as one of them.

In Germany Aunt Sara was assigned a job in a convent and I, as her daughter, was allowed to stay with her. But because I wasn't German, I couldn't go to school or eat with the children. Instead I cut beans and served the meals.

Three days after we arrived, the SS came to the convent to arrest us. As we were being dragged out, the nuns wondered what was going on. And we wondered who could have turned us in.

For six hours the Gestapo questioned us at their headquarters, accusing us of being Jewish. But Aunt Sara and I insisted we weren't. Then an SS man took me into the corridor and pointed a revolver at my head. "If you tell me you're Jewish, I'll let you go," he said. But I refused to be tricked.

Finally he made me recite Catholic prayers to prove I was Christian. I remembered them from when my Polish maid had taken me to church with her, and rattled them off. I so convinced the SS man, he let Aunt Sara and me go free. But every day the SS called the convent to see if we were still there.

In January 1945 the Americans and British started bombing the area. Although I was happy the Allies had come, I thought now we'd really be killed. Then one day in April it was quiet outside. Cautiously everyone crawled out of the shelter. The Germans were gone and the road was filled with Russian soldiers. I felt as though the Messiah had come. For the first time since the war had begun, I knew I was going to live.

That day Aunt Sara and I started back to Poland, where the war had ended a few months before. When we got there, we went to my grandfather's house, hoping my parents and sister would be waiting. Instead, Polish people were living in the house. They said we should leave the town quickly because **anti-Semitic**[8] Poles were killing Jews in large numbers.

We had no money and nowhere to stay. Aunt Sara decided to put me in an orphanage until she got settled.

---

[8] **anti-Semitic**—hostile and prejudiced against Jews.

I had never been sick all the time I had been in the coop, but in the orphanage I caught measles and then whooping cough.

Meanwhile I kept reading the lists posted in the yard to see if my parents' and sister's names were among those who had survived the concentration camps. But none of them was ever mentioned.

That November Aunt Sara came for me, and together we went to a displacement camp in the American sector of Germany. Before we left Poland, we said good-bye to Mrs. Cicha. She told us she had been sent to Auschwitz and the family who had hidden Mala had been denounced by their neighbors and sent there too. They all had survived, but not Mala, who was shot by the Germans almost as soon as she arrived in the camp. Later I learned from a cousin who had been with my parents that they too had died.

Now there was no reason for Aunt Sara and me to stay in Europe, so we applied to go to the United States. It took six years for us to get our papers. During that time I lived in the displaced persons' camp and went to school. I never saw Mrs. Cicha again.

POSTSCRIPT

When I came to the United States, I wrote to Mrs. Cicha, and over the years I sent her letters and photos of myself with my husband and three children. She always wrote back and sent pictures of herself and the house where I had been hidden.

I never asked her why she had taken such an enormous risk hiding me and all the others. I know it wasn't for the money. And it wasn't because she particularly liked Jews. She could have taken them or left them.

I think she was the kind of person who did what she believed and wasn't influenced by others. She had guts.

If it wasn't for her, a rare individual, and God watching over me, I wouldn't be here today.

Mrs. Cicha has been honored at Yad Vashem,[9] and when she was alive, the State of Israel sent her money to make her life easier. She died a few years ago.

Rose owns a video store and works there.

---

[9] *Yad Vashem*—a memorial and research organization in Israel devoted to the study of the Holocaust.

QUESTIONS TO CONSIDER

1. What factors helped Rose's family hide some of their members?

2. If you had been her parents, would you have done things differently or the same? Why?

3. What were the risks for Christians who helped to hide Jews?

War in Europe

Battle of the Bulge During the Battle of the Bulge, U.S. troops braved the weather and the enemy.

▲

Nazis in Vienna Nazi forces were welcomed by their supporters across Europe before the outbreak of the war.

Hitler in Berlin Hitler drew huge crowds in support of his rebuilding of Germany. Here Hitler is being welcomed in the streets of Berlin on May 1, 1934. ▶

◀ **Enigma** German soliders used a machine called Enigma to code messages. It required three persons to operate: one person typed, one read letters that lighted up on it, and a third wrote down the letters as they were read.

Bombing Missions Bombing missions during the war had carefully selected targets. Here the navigator of a "Flying Fortress" bomber prepares for a bombing mission.

▼

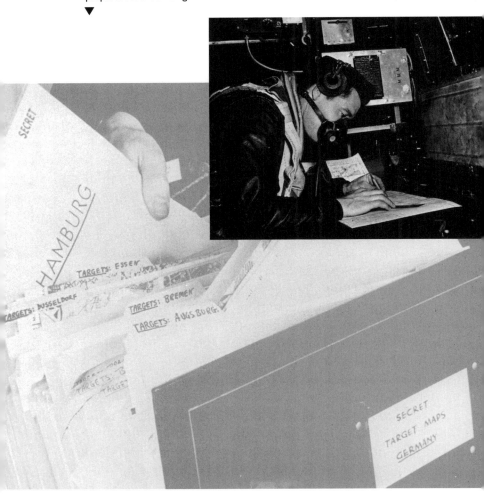

Troop Advances Because artillery often bombarded enemy positions ahead of troop advances, cities and town were reduced almost to rubble.

In towns, troops advanced building by building, flushing out the enemy.

Artillery Mobile howitzer artillery played an important role in the advancement of American troops throughout the war. Often howitzers rained fire upon enemy positions, and then the ground troops advanced.
▼

▲

Fatigue Many soldiers later described the overhwelming fatigue they so often felt during the war.

Heroes True heroes emerged from the war, such as this soldier who escaped after killing twenty Nazi soldiers by playing dead. ▶

Air Spy: The Story of Photo Intelligence in World War II

BY CONSTANCE BABINGTON-SMITH

Military intelligence is crucial to warfare. In the Second World War, as in others, all parties used the latest technology to get information about the plans and activities of their enemies. In this account, Constance Babington-Smith, daughter of the Scottish duke of Elgin, tells of her experiences as an interpreter of the photographs taken by military spy planes.

"The photographs showed. . . ." In almost every account of the Second World War, whether from the viewpoint of Air Force, Navy, or Army, these words recur again and again. For during the last war, the searching eye of the aerial camera became, to the Allies, much more than an important tactical adjunct to military operations, which had previously been its accepted wartime role. During the years between 1939 and 1945, a new kind of photographic reconnaissance,[1] strategic as well as tactical, came into being, carried out first from Britain, and then from Allied bases all over the world. The intelligence it yielded gave answers of a rapidity, scope, and accuracy which had never before been envisaged.

Behind the words "the photographs showed . . ." there is a story which is essentially twofold; for this new intelligence was the product of two extremely different activities: the taking of the pictures and the reading of their meaning. In the records of flying achievement, the photographic pilots have hitherto received little acclaim; but in many ways their work was even more demanding than that of the bomber and fighter pilots; for normally they flew alone and unarmed to their targets, and even after the photographs were taken, often from five miles up, the job was only half done: the sortie[2] was wasted unless they got the pictures back safely.

Even when the pilot was back, however, his films meant nothing without the interpreters. Many [military photographs] may arouse the comment, "I can see for myself what is of military interest without having to be called an interpreter"; and it is quite true that certain things of military interest can be recognized by anyone in certain pictures. But the vast majority of the war's aerial photographs were taken from great heights and from immediately above, and the wealth of information they hold has meaning only for the initiated. Indeed, their secret language may be compared to the language of X-ray photographs, which can be fully understood only by an eye which is experienced and a mind that has been specially trained.

---

[1] reconnaissance—a military exploration of enemy territory.

[2] sortie—the round trip of an aircraft on a combat mission.

[In] a row of little mock-Tudor villas, shabby and draughty from the bombing . . . for fifteen shivering days from December 1, 1940, five W.A.A.F.s[3] and one rather embarrassed young Army officer applied themselves to learning how to interpret aerial photographs. I was one of the W.A.A.F.s.

We sat in our greatcoats in a sparsely furnished upstairs room, and took down notes while Douglas Kendall, in his quiet emphatic way, kindled our interest in the dimensions and **armament**[4] of German battleships, and chalked up one after another the plan views of the Channel ports. I was amazed that he knew them all by heart.

For our first exercise we were given some "verticals" (photograph taken from vertically above), and gradually we learned how to recognize such major landmarks as railway stations and airfields, and to distinguish between railways, with their invariable gentle curves, and roads, which usually follow the lie of the land.

There are always shadows on daytime high-altitude photographs, because the pictures could not have been taken except from a clear sky; and I learned how much easier it is to look at the prints if you place them with the shadows falling toward you; as though the sun were shining down on the photograph from beyond the table you're working at. We could have done with some sunshine in that freezing room, where the sputtering gas fire seemed to give out more noise than heat.

Shipping was of course the first priority, and we practiced making accurate counts, listing the vessels by size—large, medium, and small. We didn't yet know enough about recognition points to identify many types.

---

[3] W.A.A.F.s—Women's Auxiliary Air Force members.
[4] **armament**—arms and equipment.

I myself was much looking forward to seeing some German aircraft, because I was intensely keen about aviation and had been writing for *The Aeroplane* for some years before the war. But the first aerial photograph of an enemy airfield I ever saw was a disappointment and shock. It was a busy fighter base in the Pas de Calais, and I had to try and count the aircraft; but even under a magnifying glass the Me 109s were no bigger than pinheads, in fact rather smaller. My heart sank, and I thought, "I shall never be able to do this." A bit later, however, we had an aircraft test which was more to my taste: we were given some good clear photographs of a dump of French aircraft which the Germans had written off at Merignac, near Bordeaux, and had to identify as many as we could, with the help of some recognition silhouettes. I thoroughly enjoyed myself but was rather worried because when I took my list to Kendall there was one airplane I hadn't been able to name. Kendall smiled. "No," he said. "Nor can I."

We started by looking at single prints, but were soon trying to use a stereoscope, that apparently simple optical instrument which presents exaggerated height and depth—if the "pair" of photographs below it is set in just the right position. There were not enough stereoscopes to go round, and I realized that a "stereo" was something important and precious. In time I borrowed one. It was an absurdly uncomplicated little gadget; something like a pair of spectacles mounted in a single rectangular piece of metal, supported by four metal legs that held it a few inches above the photographs. I stood it above a pair of prints as I had seen some of the others doing. I could see two images, not one, and there really did not seem much point. It was much simpler to work with an ordinary magnifying glass. I edged the two prints backward and forward a bit—still two images; and then suddenly the thing happened, the images fused, and the buildings in the photograph shot up toward me so that I almost drew back. It was the same sort of feeling of triumph and wonder that I remember long ago when I first stayed up on a bicycle without someone holding on behind. From then on interpretation was much easier.

Toward the end of the **fortnight**,[5] Michael Spender came and gave us a talk about the interpretation of shipping. In his hesitant but intimidating voice he spoke of the principles that apply to all interpretation.

"You must know at a glance what is normal, and then you can recognize the abnormal when you see it. When we saw the Dutch shipyards crowded with barges having their bows cut away, we knew the importance of what was happening *because* we had already been watching the normal life of those yards. And because we knew the normal look of the Channel ports we could recognize the abnormal the moment the barges started appearing there. An interpreter is like a motorist driving through a town, who suddenly sees a rubber ball bouncing across the road from a side street. He can't *see* any children playing, but he knows in a flash they are there and his brake is on. You must know what is normal, but you must also know the significance of what you see when you see it."

We listened enthralled to this **farouche**[6] flight lieutenant, who knew so much and expected so much; but his wonderful ideas did not really seem to bear much relation to our little exercises of counting and identifying.

The climax of the course, on which our fate depended, was an oral examination by Peter Riddell. We were much in awe of the dark, busy squadron leader who looked in occasionally for a quick word with Kendall.

---

[5] **fortnight**—a two-week period.
[6] **farouche**—fierce, shy.

We knew that he could not tolerate inefficiency, and we trembled as we thought how inefficient we were.

The night before the exam I sat on my bed in my Wembley **billet**,[7] forgetful of the thud of bombs, and went over and over the **silhouettes**[8]—*Bismarck, Tirpitz, Prinz Eugen* . . . shipping was my weakest subject. And then finally I consoled myself by reading a letter which had just come from a trusted friend in the R.A.F.

> I haven't the least doubt that you will sail through your present course with flying colours—but if, by some fickle chance, things don't go quite as you had hoped, don't take it too hardly. I am told that photographic interpretation requires a peculiar mentality—a kind of super jig-saw mind—which bears no relation to brains or ability.

Well, by the next evening it would be all over.

The following afternoon Riddell appeared without any ceremony and sat on a table while he shot questions at us. "How do you tell the difference between a naval unit and a merchant vessel?" he asked me.

I was paralyzed—Oh, why hadn't he asked me the wing span of a German airplane? He turned to my neighbor, Eve Holiday, and asked gently, "Do *you* know?" Eve did know and had been waiting eagerly.

"A merchant vessel is like an oblong box with pointed ends, and a naval unit is a very elongated oval—*cigar-shaped*." She drew a cigar shape in the air to stress her point. Oh yes, of course, I knew quite well really.

Next it was the turn of a W.A.A.F. with a long little face and the fragile look of a wild flower—Ann McKnight-Kauffer, daughter of the famous poster artist.

---

[7] **billet**—lodging for soldiers.

[8] **silhouettes**—outline drawings.

"In the German Army are there more mechanized divisions or horse-drawn?" Riddell asked her.

It was rather a catch question, and Ann was caught. "M-m-mechanized, I *think*," she replied.

And so it went on. We were certain we had all failed. But in fact that fifth training course at Wembley was the first on which every one of the candidates got through.

So it was in January 1941 that I took my place on one of the Second Phase shifts, twelve hours on and twenty-four hours off alternately. Wearing my new uniform with the almost invisibly thin stripe of an assistant section officer, I worked alongside a kind and cheerful Australian W.A.A.F. officer called Jean Starling. I had to tackle shipping quite often, but as all the others preferred it, and I much preferred aircraft, I more often got the airfields.

. . . I was rather taken aback, however, to find that the aircraft themselves were normally reported rather as an afterthought, at the end of the statement on the airfield itself. Surely this was putting the cart before the horse—or rather the stage before the play that was being acted? But it was hardly for a W.A.A.F. who had been an officer only a few weeks to say so.

QUESTIONS TO CONSIDER

1. According to Babington-Smith, why is military intelligence important to the war effort?

2. How, if at all, does her account change your idea of what a "soldier" is? Was Babington-Smith a "soldier" in your opinion?

Lessons of the War

BY HENRY REED

Military recruits in every country that fought in the war were put through rigorous training. English poet Henry Reed (1914–1986) was fascinated by the rhythms of the language used with new soldiers, especially its humorous aspects. Reed's friends enjoyed his imitations of training sergeants. This excerpt is from his poem, "Lessons of the War."

1. NAMING OF PARTS

Today we have naming of parts. Yesterday,
We had daily cleaning. And tomorrow morning,
We shall have what to do after firing. But today,
Today we have naming of parts. Japonica[1]
Glistens like coral in all of the neighbouring gardens,
      And today we have naming of parts.

---

[1] Japonica—a flowering shrub with bright red blossoms.

58   **World War II**

This is the lower sling swivel. And this
Is the upper sling swivel, whose use you will see,
When you are given your slings. And this is the
    piling swivel,
Which in your case you have not got. The branches
Hold in the gardens their silent, eloquent gestures,
            Which in our case we have not got.

This is the safety-catch, which is always released
With an easy flick of the thumb. And please do not let me
See anyone using his finger. You can do it quite easy
If you have any strength in your thumb. The blossoms
Are fragile and motionless, never letting anyone see
            Any of them using their finger.

And this you can see is the bolt. The purpose of this
Is to open the breech, as you see. We can slide it
Rapidly backwards and forwards: we call this
Easing the spring.[2] And rapidly backwards and
    forwards
The early bees are assaulting and fumbling the flowers:
            They call it easing the Spring.

They call it easing the Spring: it is perfectly easy
If you have any strength in your thumb; like the bolt,
And the breech, and the cocking-piece, and the point
    of balance,
Which in our case we have not got; and the almond
    blossom
Silent in all of the gardens and the bees going backwards
    and forwards,
            For today we have naming of parts.

---

[2] spring—when the rifle bolt is slid, bullets are ejected, which takes pressure
off the spring on the ammunition chamber.

2. JUDGING DISTANCES

Not only how far away, but the way that you say it
Is very important. Perhaps you may never get
The knack of judging a distance, but at least you know
How to report on a landscape: the central sector,
The right of arc and that, which we had last Tuesday,
        And at least you know

That maps are of time,[3] not place, so far as the army
Happens to be concerned—the reason being,
Is one which need not delay us. Again, you know
There are three kinds of tree, three only, the fir and
   the poplar,
And those which have bushy tops to; and lastly
        That things only seem to be things.

A barn is not called a barn, to put it more plainly,
Or a field in the distance, where sheep may be safely
   grazing.
You must never be over-sure. You must say, when
   reporting:
At five o'clock in the central sector is a dozen
Of what appear to be animals; whatever you do,
        Don't call the bleeders *sheep.*

---

[3] time—Reed is referring to the military custom of describing the location of places by reference to an imaginary clock. See how the sheep are located in the following stanza.

I am sure that's quite clear; and suppose, for the sake
   of example,
The one at the end, asleep, endeavours to tell us
What he sees over there to the west, and how far away,
After first having come to attention. There to the west,
On the fields of summer the sun and the shadows
   bestow
         Vestments of purple and gold.

The still white dwellings are like a mirage in the heat,
And under the swaying elms a man and a woman
Lie gently together. Which is, perhaps, only to say
That there is a row of houses to the left of arc,
And that under some poplars a pair of what appear
   to be humans
         Appear to be loving.

Well that, for an answer, is what we might rightly call
Moderately satisfactory only, the reason being,
Is that two things have been omitted, and those are
   important.
The human beings, now: in what direction are they,
And how far away, would you say? And do not forget
         There may be dead ground[4] in between.

There may be dead ground in between; and I may not
   have got
The knack of judging a distance; I will only venture
A guess that perhaps between me and the apparent lovers
(Who, incidentally, appear by now to have finished,)
At seven o'clock from the houses, is roughly a distance
   . Of about one year and a half.

---

[4] dead ground—a military term for an area that cannot be hit with the fire of
a given weapon from a given spot.

3. UNARMED COMBAT

In due course of course you will all be issued with
Your proper issue; but until tomorrow,
You can hardly be said to need it; and until that time,
We shall have unarmed combat. I shall teach you
The various holds and rolls and throws and breakfalls
    Which you may sometimes meet.

And the various holds and rolls and throws and
   breakfalls
Do not depend on any sort of weapon,
But only on what I might coin a phrase and call
The ever-important question of human balance,
And the ever-important need to be in a strong
    Position at the start.

There are many kinds of weakness about the body,
Where you would least expect, like the ball of the foot.
But the various holds and rolls and throws and
   breakfalls
Will always come in useful. And never be frightened
To tackle from behind: it may not be clean to do so,
    But this is global war.

QUESTIONS TO CONSIDER

1. What two things does Reed compare in his poem? What do you think the comparison highlights?

2. What seems to be Reed's attitude toward the war? Cite specific lines in the poem to support your answer.

3. What do you think is the point or idea of the last section titled "Unarmed Combat"?

I Forgot for a Moment

BY EDNA ST. VINCENT MILLAY

Yearning for the time before Hitler (the "harsh foreign voice" referred to in this poem) broke his promises of peace and overran Europe, poet Edna St. Vincent Millay (1892–1950) wrote this in July 1940.

July 1940
I forgot for a moment France; I forgot England; I forgot
    my care:
I lived for a moment in a world where I was free to be
With the things and people that I love, and I was
    happy there.
I forgot for a moment Holland, I forgot my heavy care.

I lived for a moment in a world so lovely, so inept
At twisted words and crooked deeds, it was as if I
    slept and dreamt.

It seemed that all was well with Holland—not a tank had crushed
The tulips there.
Mile after mile the level lowlands blossomed—yellow square, white square,
Scarlet strip and mauve strip bright beneath the brightly clouded sky, the round clouds and the gentle air.
Along the straight canals between striped fields of tulips in the morning sailed
Broad ships, their hulls by tulip-beds concealed, only the sails showing.

It seemed that all was well with England—the harsh foreign voice[1] hysterically vowing,
Once more, to keep its word, at length was disbelieved, and hushed.

It seemed that all was well with France, with her straight roads
Lined with slender poplars, and the peasants on the skyline ploughing.

---

[1] "harsh foreign voice"—refers to Hilter's voice.

QUESTIONS TO CONSIDER

1. What does Millay mean when she says, "I forgot . . . France, . . . England, . . . Holland"?

2. What do the lines that describe a world "inept at twisted words and crooked deeds" mean?

3. What did the war do to the patterns that Millay describes? In your opinion, do you think her poem is mostly about war or something else?

Second Air Force

BY RANDALL JARRELL

*American poet Randall Jarrell (1914–1965) was born in Nashville,
Tennessee. He was trained as an army air force pilot and as a
control operator. In "Second Air Force," a woman is visiting her
soldier son. The poet describes what inspired his poem by having
her remember a newspaper article that depicted a conversation
between a bomber, in flames over Germany, and one of the
fighters protecting it. "Then I heard the bomber call me in, 'Little
Friend, Little Friend, I got two engines on fire. Can you see me,
Little Friend?' I said, 'I'm crossing right over you. Let's go home.'"*

Far off, above the plain the summer dries,
The great loops of the hangars sway like hills.
Buses and weariness and loss, the nodding soldiers
Are wire, the bare frame building, and a pass
To what was hers; her head hides his square patch
And she thinks heavily: My son is grown.
She sees a world: sand roads, tar-paper barracks,
The bubbling asphalt of the runways, sage,
The dunes rising to the interminable ranges,
The dim flights moving over clouds like clouds.

The armorers[1] in their patched faded green,
Sweat-stiffened, banded with brass cartridges,
Walk to the line; their Fortresses,[2] all tail,
Stand wrong and flimsy on their skinny legs,
And the crews climb to them clumsily as bears.
The head withdraws into its hatch (a boy's),
The engines rise to their blind laboring roar,
And the green, made beasts run home to air.
Now in each aspect death is pure.
(At twilight they wink over men like stars
And hour by hour, through the night, some see
The great lights floating in—from Mars, from Mars.)
How emptily the watchers see them gone.

They go, there is silence; the woman and her son
Stand in the forest of the shadows, and the light
Washes them like water. In the long-sunken city
Of evening, the sunlight stills like sleep
The faint wonder of the drowned; in the evening,
In the last dreaming light, so fresh, so old,
The soldiers pass like beasts, unquestioning,
And the watcher for an instant understands
What there is then no need to understand;
But she wakes from her knowledge, and her stare,
A shadow now, moves emptily among
The shadows learning in their shadowy fields
The empty missions.
                    Remembering,
She hears the bomber calling, *Little Friend!*
To the fighter hanging in the hostile sky,
And sees the ragged flame eat, rib by rib,
Along the metal of the wing into her heart:
The lives stream out, blossom, and float steadily
To the flames of the earth, the flames
That burn like stars above the lands of men.

---

[1] armorers—people who make, test, and repair firearms.

[2] Fortresses—short for Flying Fortresses, a type of bomber used in World War II.

She saves from the twilight that takes everything
A squadron shipping, in its last parade—
Its dogs run by it, barking at the band—
A gunner walking to his barracks, half-asleep,
Starting at something, stumbling (above, invisible,
The crews in the steady winter of the sky
Tremble in their wired fur); and feels for them
The love of life for life. The hopeful cells
Heavy with someone else's death, cold carriers
Of someone else's victory, grope past their lives
Into her own bewilderment: The years meant *this?*

But for them the bombers answer everything.

QUESTIONS TO CONSIDER

1. What aspect of war do you think Jarrell is trying to highlight? Why?

2. Why do you think he focuses on the image of a plane in flames "in the hostile sky"?

War in Europe
and Africa

The Atlantic Charter

In August of 1941, President Franklin D. Roosevelt and Prime Minister Winston Churchill held a secret three-day meeting in Newfoundland. Although the U.S. was still technically neutral at this time, the two leaders shared their goals for the war and for the time after it was over. Churchill, for instance, agreed to give up British rule over the countries it had colonized in the previous century. After the meeting, they issued the Atlantic Charter specifically to make their mutual war goals clear.

Joint declaration of the President of the United States of America and the Prime Minister, Mr. Churchill, representing His Majesty's government in the United Kingdom, being met together, deem it right to make known certain common principles in the national policies of their respective countries on which they base their hopes for a better future for the world.

First, their countries seek no aggrandizement, territorial or other;

Second, they desire to see no territorial changes that do not accord with the freely expressed wishes of the people concerned;

Third, they respect the right of all peoples to choose the form of government under which they will live; and they wish to see sovereign rights and self-government restored to those who have been forcibly deprived of them;

Fourth, they will endeavor, with due respect for their existing obligations; to further the enjoyment by all States, great or small, victor or vanquished, of access, on equal terms, to the trade and to the raw materials of the world which are needed for their economic prosperity;

Fifth, they desire to bring about the fullest collaboration between all nations in the economic field with the object of securing, for all, improved labor standards, economic advancement and social security;

Sixth, after the final destruction of the Nazi tyranny, they hope to see established a peace which will afford to all nations the means of dwelling in safety within their own boundaries, and which will afford assurance that all the men in all the lands may live out their lives in freedom from fear and want;

Seventh, such a peace should enable all men to traverse the high seas and oceans without hindrance;

Eighth, they believe that all of the nations of the world, for realistic as well as spiritual reasons must come to the abandonment of the use of force. Since no future peace can be maintained if land, sea or air armaments continue to be employed by nations which threaten, or may threaten aggression outside of their frontiers, they believe, pending the establishment of a wider and permanent system of general security, that the **disarmament**[1] of such nations is essential. They will likewise aid and encourage all other practicable measures which will lighten for peace-loving peoples the crushing burden of armaments.

---

[1] **disarmament**—removal of armed forces.

QUESTIONS TO CONSIDER

1. In your own words, restate the main points of the Atlantic Charter.

2. What effect do you think this document had on the different nations of the world?

3. What obstacles still stand in the way of achieving these goals?

The Battle for Stalingrad

BY WILLIAM HOFFMAN

Hitler had long planned to attack the Soviet Union, in spite of an earlier treaty in which he agreed not to do so. In 1941, Hitler's forces drove as far as the outskirts of Moscow before they were repelled. His armies encircled Leningrad and began a terrible siege that starved 1,000,000 people. Another branch of the army took Kiev. The next year, the terrible fighting continued, and both Stalin and Hitler were absolutely determined not to give up. Here a German soldier describes in his diary the battle for Stalingrad (now Volgograd) in late 1942.

Today, after we'd had a bath, the company commander told us that if our future operations are as successful, we'll soon reach the Volga, take Stalingrad and then the war will inevitably soon be over. Perhaps we'll be home by Christmas.

July 29, 1942—The company commander says the Russian troops are completely broken, and cannot hold out any longer. To reach the Volga and take Stalingrad is not so difficult for us. The Führer[1] knows where the Russians' weak point is. Victory is not far away. . . .

August 2—What great spaces the Soviets occupy, what rich fields there are to be had here after the war's over! Only let's get it over with quickly. I believe that the Führer will carry the thing through to a successful end.

August 10—The Führer's orders were read out to us. He expects victory of us. We are all convinced that they can't stop us.

August 12—We are advancing towards Stalingrad along the railway line. Yesterday Russian "katyushi"[2] and then tanks halted our **regiment**.[3] "The Russians are throwing in their last forces," Captain Werner explained to me. Large-scale help is coming up for us, and the Russians will be beaten.

This morning outstanding soldiers were presented with decorations. . . . Will I really go back to Elsa without a decoration? I believe that for Stalingrad the Führer will decorate even me. . . .

August 23—Splendid news—north of Stalingrad our troops have reached the Volga and captured part of the city. The Russians have two alternatives, either to flee across the Volga or give themselves up. Our company's interpreter has **interrogated**[4] a captured Russian officer. He was wounded, but asserted that the Russians would fight for Stalingrad to the last round. Something incomprehensible is, in fact, going on. In the north our troops capture a part of Stalingrad and reach the Volga, but in the south the doomed divisions are continuing to resist bitterly. Fanaticism. . . .

---

[1] Führer—"leader" in German, referring here to Hitler.

[2] katyushi—small rocket launchers.

[3] **regiment**—a military unit of at least two battalions.

[4] **interrogated**—formally questioned.

August 27—A continuous cannonade on all sides. We are slowly advancing. Less than twenty miles to go to Stalingrad. In the daytime we can see the smoke of fires, at nighttime the bright glow. They say that the city is on fire; on the Führer's orders our Luftwaffe[5] has sent it up in flames. That's what the Russians need, to stop them from resisting. . . .

September 4—We are being sent northward along the front towards Stalingrad. We marched all night and by dawn had reached Voroponovo Station. We can already see the smoking town. It's a happy thought that the end of the war is getting nearer. That's what everyone is saying. If only the days and nights would pass more quickly. . . .

September 5—Our regiment has been ordered to attack Sadovaya station—that's nearly in Stalingrad. Are the Russians really thinking of holding out in the city itself? We had no peace all night from the Russian artillery and aeroplanes. Lots of wounded are being brought by. God protect me. . . .

September 8—Two days of non-stop fighting. The Russians are defending themselves with insane stubbornness. Our regiment has lost many men from the "katyushi," which belch out terrible fire. I have been sent to work at battalion H.Q. It must be mother's prayers that have taken me away from the company's trenches. . . .

September 11—Our battalion is fighting in the suburbs of Stalingrad. We can already see the Volga; firing is going on all the time. Wherever you look is fire and flames. . . . Russian cannon and machine-guns are firing out of the burning city. Fanatics . . .

September 13—An unlucky number. This morning "katyushi" attacks caused the company heavy losses:

---

[5] Luftwaffe—the German air force.

twenty-seven dead and fifty wounded. The Russians are fighting desperately like wild beasts, don't give themselves up, but come up close and then throw grenades. Lieutenant Kraus was killed yesterday, and there is no company commander.

September 16—Our battalion, plus ranks, is attacking the [grain storage] elevator, from which smoke is pouring—the grain in it is burning, the Russians seem to have set light to it themselves. Barbarism. The battalion is suffering heavy losses. There are not more than sixty men left in each company. The elevator is occupied not by men but by devils that no flames or bullets can destroy.

September 18—Fighting is going on inside the elevator. The Russians inside are condemned men; the battalion commander says: "The commissars[6] have ordered those men to die in the elevator."

If all the buildings of Stalingrad are defended like this then none of our soldiers will get back to Germany. I had a letter from Elsa today. She's expecting me home when victory's won.

September 20—The battle for the elevator is still going on. The Russians are firing on all sides. We stay in our cellar; you can't go out into the street. Sergeant-Major Nuschke was killed today running across a street. Poor fellow, he's got three children.

September 22—Russian resistance in the elevator has been broken. Our troops are advancing towards the Volga. . . .

. . . Our old soldiers have never experienced such bitter fighting before.

September 26—Our regiment is involved in constant heavy fighting. After the elevator was taken the Russians continued to defend themselves just as stubbornly. You don't see them at all, they have established themselves

---

[6] commissars—Russian officers.

in houses and cellars and are firing on all sides, including from our rear—barbarians, they use gangster methods.

In the blocks captured two days ago Russian soldiers appeared from somewhere or other and fighting has flared up with fresh **vigor**.[7] Our men are being killed not only in the firing line, but in the rear, in buildings we have already occupied.

The Russians have stopped surrendering at all. If we take any prisoners it's because they are hopelessly wounded, and can't move by themselves. Stalingrad is hell. Those who are merely wounded are lucky; they will doubtless be at home and celebrate victory with their families. . . .

September 28—Our regiment, and the whole division, are today celebrating victory. Together with our tank crews we have taken the southern part of the city and reached the Volga. We paid dearly for our victory. In three weeks we have occupied about five and a half square miles. The commander has congratulated us on our victory. . . .

October 3—After marching through the night we have established ourselves in a shrub-covered gully. We are apparently going to attack the factories, the chimneys of which we can see clearly. Behind them is the Volga. We have entered a new area. It was night but we saw many crosses with our helmets on top. Have we really lost so many men? Damn this Stalingrad!

October 4—Our regiment is attacking the Barrikady settlement. A lot of Russian tommy-gunners[8] have appeared. Where are they bringing them from?

October 5—Our battalion has gone into the attack four times, and got stopped each time. Russian snipers hit anyone who shows himself carelessly from behind shelter.

---

[7] **vigor**—strength.
[8] tommy-gunners—soldiers with submachine guns.

October 10—The Russians are so close to us that our planes cannot bomb them. We are preparing for a decisive attack. The Führer has ordered the whole of Stalingrad to be taken as rapidly as possible.

October 14—It has been fantastic since morning: our aeroplanes and artillery have been hammering the Russian positions for hours on end; everything in sight is being blotted from the face of the earth. . . .

October 22—Our regiment has failed to break into the factory. We have lost many men; every time you move you have to jump over bodies. You can scarcely breathe in the daytime: there is nowhere and no one to remove the bodies, so they are left there to rot. Who would have thought three months ago that instead of the joy of victory we would have to endure such sacrifice and torture, the end of which is nowhere in sight? . . .

The soldiers are calling Stalingrad the mass grave of the Wehrmacht.[9] There are very few men left in the companies. We have been told we are soon going to be withdrawn to be brought back up to strength.

October 27—Our troops have captured the whole of the Barrikady factory, but we cannot break through to the Volga. The Russians are not men, but some kind of cast-iron creatures; they never get tired and are not afraid of fire. We are absolutely exhausted; our regiment now has barely the strength of a company. The Russian artillery at the other side of the Volga won't let you lift your head. . . .

October 28—Every soldier sees himself as a condemned man. The only hope is to be wounded and taken back to the rear. . . .

---

[9] Wehrmacht—German army.

November 3—In the last few days our battalion has several times tried to attack the Russian positions, . . . to no avail. On this sector also the Russians won't let you lift your head. There have been a number of cases of self-inflicted wounds and **malingering**[10] among the men. Every day I write two or three reports about them.

November 10—A letter from Elsa today. Everyone expects us home for Christmas. In Germany everyone believes we already hold Stalingrad. How wrong they are. If they could only see what Stalingrad has done to our army.

November 18—Our attack with ranks yesterday had no success. After our attack the field was littered with dead.

November 21—The Russians have gone over to the offensive along the whole front. Fierce fighting is going on. So, there it is—the Volga, victory and soon home to our families! We shall obviously be seeing them next in the other world.

November 29—We are encircled. It was announced this morning that the Führer has said: "The army can trust me to do everything necessary to ensure supplies and rapidly break the encirclement."

December 3—We are on hunger rations and waiting for the rescue that the Führer promised.
I send letters home, but there is no reply.

December 7—Rations have been cut to such an extent that the soldiers are suffering terribly from hunger; they are issuing one loaf of stale bread for five men.

December 11—Three questions are obsessing every soldier and officer: When will the Russians stop firing and let us sleep in peace, if only for one night? How and

---

[10] **malingering**—faking illness to avoid work or battle.

with what are we going to fill our empty stomachs, which, apart from 3 $1/2$–7 ozs of bread, receive virtually nothing at all? And when will Hitler take any decisive steps to free our armies from encirclement?

December 14—Everybody is racked with hunger. Frozen potatoes are the best meal, but to get them out of the ice-covered ground under fire from Russian bullets is not so easy.

December 18—The officers today told the soldiers to be prepared for action. General Manstein is approaching Stalingrad from the south with strong forces. This news brought hope to the soldiers' hearts. God, let it be!

December 21—We are waiting for the order, but for some reason or other it has been a long time coming. Can it be that it is not true about Manstein? This is worse than any torture.

December 23—Still no orders. It was all a bluff with Manstein. Or has he been defeated at the approaches to Stalingrad?

December 25—The Russian radio has announced the defeat of Manstein. Ahead of us is either death or captivity.

December 26—The horses have already been eaten. I would eat a cat; they say its meat is also tasty. The soldiers look like corpses or lunatics, looking for something to put in their mouths. They no longer take cover from Russian shells; they haven't the strength to walk, run away and hide. A curse on this war! . . .

QUESTIONS TO CONSIDER

1. What is Hoffman's mood in the entries through August 12?

2. What is going on that Hoffman says is "incomprehensible" on August 23?

3. How would you say Hoffman describes the Russian soldiers?

4. Consider how the Russians must have thought about the German soldiers. What words might they have used to describe them?

5. How do you think you would have reacted if you had been in Hoffman's place?

The Infantry in North Africa

BY ERNIE PYLE

The British, French, and Italians all had colonies in Africa which they had taken in the 19th century. Germany, too, had had colonies there, but these had been divided up among the victorious allies of World War I in the Treaty of Versailles. The Second World War moved into Africa as Germany sought to regain its lands there. By 1942, the Americans were fighting there in support of their allies. Ernie Pyle (1900–1945), a Pulitzer Prize-winning journalist carried by as many as 200 newspapers in the U.S., let the folks at home know what war was like through his columns. Traveling with the infantry, Pyle kept a record of their battles, lied in bunkers with them, and eventually died with them. He was shot in 1945 shortly before the end of the war by Japanese machine-gun fire, on the small island of Shima, near Okinawa in the Pacific, when he raised his head from a trench to see what was going on.

AT THE FRONT LINES IN TUNISIA, *May 1, 1943*— When our infantry[1] goes into a big push in northern

---

[1] infantry—the combat units that fight on foot.

Tunisia each man is issued three bars of D-ration chocolate, enough to last one day. He takes no other food.

He carries two canteens of water instead of the usual one. He carries no blankets. He leaves behind all extra clothes except his raincoat. In his pockets he may have a few toilet articles. Some men carry their money. Others give it to friends to keep.

In the days that follow they live in a way that is inconceivable to us at home. They walk and fight all night without sleep. Next day they lie flat in foxholes,[2] or hide in fields of freshly green, knee-high wheat.

If they're in the fields they dare not even move enough to dig foxholes, for that would bring the German artillery. They can't rise even for nature's calls. The German feels for them continually with his artillery.

The slow drag of these motionless daylight hours is nearly unendurable. Lt. Mickey Miller of Morgantown, Indiana, says this lifeless waiting in a wheatfield is almost the worst part of the whole battle.

The second evening after the attack begins, C-rations[3] and five-gallon cans of water are brought up across country in jeeps, after dark. You eat in the dark, and you can't see the can you are eating from. You just eat by feel. You make cold coffee from cold water.

One night a German shell landed close and fragments punctured fifteen cans of water.

Each night enough canned rations for three meals are brought up, but when the men move on after supper most of them either lose or leave behind the next day's rations, because they're too heavy to carry. But, as they say, when you're in battle and excited you sort of go on your nerve. You don't think much about being hungry.

The men fight at night and lie low by day, when the artillery takes over its blasting job. Weariness gradually creeps over them. What sleeping they do is in daytime.

---

[2] foxholes—shallow pits that soldiers dig for protection from enemy fire.

[3] C-rations—food issued to soldiers.

But, as they say, at night it's too cold and in daytime it's too hot. Also the fury of the artillery[4] makes daytime sleeping next to impossible. So does the heat of the sun. Some men have passed out from heat prostration. Many of them get upset stomachs from the heat.

But as the third and fourth days roll on weariness overcomes all obstacles to sleep. Men who sit down for a moment's rest fall asleep in the grass. There are even men who say they can march while asleep.

Lt. Col. Charlie Stone of New Brunswick, New Jersey, actually went to sleep while standing up talking on a field telephone—not while listening, but in the middle of a spoken sentence.

When sometimes they do lie down at night the men have only their raincoats to lie on. It is cold, and the dew makes the grass as wet as rain. They don't dare start a fire to heat their food, even in daytime, for the smoke would attract enemy fire. At night they can't even light cigarettes in the open, so after digging their foxholes they get down and make hoods over their heads with their raincoats, and light up under the coats.

They have plenty of cigarettes. Those who run out during battle are supplied by others. Every night new supplies of water and C-rations are brought up in jeeps.

IN THE FRONT LINES BEFORE MATEUR, *Northern Tunisia, May 2, 1943*—We're now with an infantry outfit that has battled ceaselessly for four days and nights.

This northern warfare has been in the mountains. You don't ride much anymore. It is walking and climbing and crawling country. The mountains aren't big, but they are constant. They are largely treeless. They are easy to defend and bitter to take. But we are taking them.

---

[4] artillery—large weapons, such as cannons and missile launchers, that are operated by crews, to shoot long-range at the enemy.

The Germans lie on the back slope of every ridge, deeply dug into foxholes. In front of them the fields and pastures are hideous with thousands of hidden mines. The forward slopes are left open, **untenanted**,[5] and if the Americans tried to scale these slopes they would be murdered wholesale in an inferno of machine-gun crossfire plus mortars and grenades.

Consequently we don't do it that way. We have fallen back to the old warfare of first **pulverizing**[6] the enemy with artillery, then sweeping around the ends of the hill with infantry and taking them from the sides and behind.

I've written before how the big guns crack and roar almost constantly throughout the day and night. They lay a screen ahead of our troops. By magnificent shooting they drop shells on the back slopes. By means of shells timed to burst in the air a few feet from the ground, they get the Germans even in their foxholes. Our troops have found that the Germans dig foxholes down and then under, trying to get cover from the shell bursts that shower death from above.

Our artillery has really been sensational. For once we have enough of something and at the right time. Officers tell me they actually have more guns than they know what to do with.

All the guns in any one sector can be centered to shoot at one spot. And when we lay the whole business on a German hill the whole slope seems to erupt. It becomes an unbelievable **cauldron**[7] of fire and smoke and dirt. Veteran German soldiers say they have never been through anything like it.

Now to the infantry . . .

I love the infantry because they are the underdogs. They are the mud-rain-frost-and-wind boys. They have

---

[5] **untenanted**—without people.

[6] **pulverizing**—to pound, grind, or crush into dust through relentless bombardment.

[7] **cauldron**—a very large cooking pot used for boiling soup (here used figuratively).

no comforts, and they even learn to live without the necessities. And in the end they are the guys that wars can't be won without.

I wish you could see just one of the **ineradicable**[8] pictures I have in my mind today. In this particular picture I am sitting among clumps of sword-grass on a steep and rocky hillside that we have just taken. We are looking out over a vast rolling country to the rear.

A narrow path comes like a ribbon over a hill miles away, down a long slope, across a creek, up a slope and over another hill.

All along the length of this ribbon there is now a thin line of men. For four days and nights they have fought hard, eaten little, washed none, and slept hardly at all. Their nights have been violent with attack, fright, butchery, and their days sleepless and miserable with the crash of artillery.

The men are walking. They are fifty feet apart, for dispersal. Their walk is slow, for they are dead weary, as you can tell even when looking at them from behind. Every line and sag of their bodies speaks their inhuman exhaustion.

On their shoulders and backs they carry heavy steel tripods, machine-gun barrels, leaden boxes of ammunition. Their feet seem to sink into the ground from the overload they are bearing.

They don't slouch. It is the terrible deliberation of each step that spells out their appalling tiredness. Their faces are black and unshaven. They are young men, but the grime and whiskers and exhaustion make them look middle-aged.

In their eyes as they pass is not hatred, not excitement, not despair, not the tonic of their victory—there is just the simple expression of being here as though they had been here doing this forever, and nothing else.

---

[8] **ineradicable**—not capable of being erased.

The line moves on, but it never ends. All afternoon men keep coming round the hill and vanishing eventually over the horizon. It is one long tired line of antlike men.

There is an agony in your heart and you almost feel ashamed to look at them. They are just guys from Broadway and Main Street, but you wouldn't remember them. They are too far away now. They are too tired. Their world can never be known to you, but if you could see them just once, just for an instant, you would know that no matter how hard people work back home they are not keeping pace with these infantrymen in Tunisia.

INTERMISSION

IN THE FRONT LINES BEFORE MATEUR, *May 3, 1943*—After four days in battle the famous infantry outfit that I'm with sat on its newly won hill and took two days' rest while companion units on each side of it leap-frogged ahead.

The men dig in on the back slope of the hill before any rest begins. Everybody digs in. This is an **inviolate**[9] rule of the commanding officers and nobody wants to disobey it. Every time you pause, even if you think you're dying of weariness, you dig yourself a hole before you sit down. . . .

The startling thing to me about these rest periods is how quickly the human body can recuperate from critical exhaustion, how rapidly the human mind snaps back to the normal state of laughing, grousing, yarn-spinning, and yearning for home.

Here is what happens when a unit stops to rest.

My unit stops just after daybreak on Hill 394. Foxholes are dug, outposts placed, phone wires strung on the ground. Some patrol work goes on as usual. Then the men lie down and sleep till the blistering heat of the sun wakes them up.

---

[9] **inviolate**—unbroken.

After that you sit around in bunches recounting things. You don't do much of anything. The day just easily kills itself.

That first evening is when life begins to seem like Christmas Eve. The mail comes up in jeeps just before dark. Then comes the men's blanket rolls. At dark, hot food arrives—the first hot food in four days.

This food is cooked in rotting kitchens several miles back and brought up by jeep, in big thermos containers, to the foot of the hill. Men carry the containers, slung on poles over their shoulders, up goat paths in the darkness to all parts of the mountain.

Hot food and hot coffee put life in a man, and then in a pathetic kind of contentment, you lie down and you sleep. The all-night crash of the artillery behind you is completely unheard through your weariness.

There are no mosquitoes so far in the mountains, and very few fleas, but there are lots of ants.

Hot food arrives again in the morning, before daylight. You eat breakfast at four A.M. Then begins a day of reassembling yourself.

Word is passed that mail will be collected that evening, so the boys sit on the ground and write letters. But writing is hard, for they can't tell in their letters what they've just been through.

The men put water in their steel helmets and wash and shave for the first time in days. A few men at a time are sent to the creek in the valley to take baths. The remainder sit in groups on the ground talking, or individually in foxholes cleaning their guns, reading, or just relaxing.

A two-months-old batch of copies of the magazine *Yank* arrives, and a two-weeks-old bunch of the *Stars and Stripes*. Others read detective magazines and comic books that have come up with their bedrolls.

At noon everybody opens cans of cold C-ration. Cold coffee in five-gallon water cans is put in the sun to warm.

Soldiers cut each other's hair. It doesn't matter how it looks, for they aren't going anywhere fancy, anyhow. Some of them strip nearly naked and lie on their blankets for a sunbath. By now their bodies are tanned as though they had been wintering at Miami Beach. They wear the inner part of their helmets, for the noonday sun is dangerous.

Their knees are skinned from crawling over rocks. They find little unimportant injuries that they didn't know they had. Some take off their shoes and socks and look over their feet, which are violently purple with athlete's-foot ointment.

I sit around with them, and they get to telling stories, both funny and serious, about their battle. They are all disappointed when they learn I am not permitted to name the outfit they're in, for they are all proud of it and would like the folks at home to know what they've done.

"We always get it the toughest," they say. "This is our third big battle now since coming to Africa. The Jerry[10] is really afraid of us now. He knows what outfit we are, and he doesn't like us."

Thus they talk and boast and laugh and speak of fear. Evening draws down and the chill sets in once more. Hot chow arrives just after dusk.

And then the word is passed around. Orders have come by telephone.

There is no excitement, no grouching, no eagerness either. They had expected it.

Quietly they roll their packs, strap them on, lift their rifles and fall into line.

There is not a sound as they move like **wraiths**[11] in single file down tortuous goat paths, walking slowly, feeling the ground with their toes, stumbling and

---

[10] Jerry—the English slang name for a German soldier.
[11] **wraiths**—living people who appear ghost-like and near death.

hushfully cussing. They will walk all night and attack before dawn.

They move like ghosts. You don't hear or see them three feet away. Now and then a light flashes lividly from a blast by our big guns, and then for just an instant you see a long slow line of dark-helmeted forms silhouetted in the flash.

Then darkness and silence consume them again, and somehow you are terribly moved.

THE END IN TUNISIA

TUNISIAN FRONT, *May 7, 1943*—The thing that Americans in Africa had fought and worked six months to get came today. When it did come, it was an avalanche almost impossible to describe. The flood of prisoners choked the roads. There were acres of captured materials.

I'll try to tell you what the spirit of the day was like.

It was a holiday, though everybody kept on working. Everybody felt suddenly free inside, as though personal worry had been lifted. It was like the way we used to feel as children on the farm, when parents surprised us by saying work was finished and we were going to the state fair for a day. And when you have looked, goggle-eyed, all day, at more Germans than you ever expected to see in your life, you really feel as if you have been to a fair.

Today you saw Germans walking alone along highways. You saw them riding, stacked up in our jeeps, with one lone American driver. You saw them by hundreds, crammed as in a subway in their own trucks, with their own drivers. And in the forward areas our fairgrounds of mile after mile contained more Germans than Americans. Germans were everywhere.

It made you a little lightheaded to stand in the center of a crowd, the only American among scores of German soldiers, and not have to feel afraid of them. Their 88's stood abandoned. In the fields dead Germans still lay on the grass. By the roadside scores of tanks and trucks still burned. Dumps flamed, and German command posts lay littered where they had tried to wreck as much as possible before surrendering.

But all those were sideshows—the big show was the mass of men in strange uniforms, lining roads, swamping farmyards, blackening fields, waiting for us to tell them where to go.

High German officers were obviously down in the mouth over the tragic end of their campaign. We saw some tears. Officers wept over the ghastly death toll taken of their men during the last few days. Officers were **meticulously**[12] correct in their military behavior, but otherwise standoffish and silent.

Not so the common soldiers. I mingled with them all day and sensed no sadness among them. Theirs was not the delight of the Italians, but rather an acceptance of defeat in a war well-fought—why be surly about it?

They were friendly, very friendly. Being prisoners, it obviously paid them to be friendly; yet their friendliness seemed genuine. Just as when the French and Americans first met, the Germans started learning English words and teaching us German words.

But circumstances didn't permit much **communion**[13] between them and our troops. Those Americans who came in direct contact with them gave necessary orders and herded them into trucks. All other Americans just stared curiously as they passed. I saw very little **fraternizing**[14] with prisoners.

I saw no acts of **belligerence**[15] and heard neither boos nor cheers. But I did hear a hundred times: "This is the way it should be. Now we can go on from here."

German boys were as curious about us as we were about them. Every time I stopped, a crowd would form

---

[12] **meticulously**—most precisely.

[13] **communion**—togetherness.

[14] **fraternizing**—friendly or brotherly interaction with the enemy or opposing group.

[15] **belligerence**—hostile acts or attitudes.

quickly. In almost every group was one who spoke English. In all honesty I can't say their bearing or personality was a bit different from that of a similar bunch of American prisoners. They gave us their cigarettes and accepted ours. They examined the jeep, and asked questions about our uniforms. If you passed one walking alone, usually he would smile and speak.

One high American officer told me he found himself feeling sorry for them—until he remembered how they had killed so many of his men with their sneaking mines, how they had him pinned down a few days ago with bullets flying; then he hated them.

I am always a sucker for the guy who loses, but somehow it never occurred to me today to feel sorry for those prisoners. They didn't give you a feeling they needed any sorrowing over. They were loyal to their country and sorry they lost but, now that it was over for them, they personally seemed glad to be out of it.

Tonight they still lounge by thousands in fields along the roads. Our trucks, and theirs too, are not sufficient to haul them away. They will just have to wait their turn to be taken off to prison camps. No guards are necessary to keep them from running off into the darkness tonight. They have already done their running and now they await our pleasure, rather humbly and with a curious eagerness to see what comes next for them.

QUESTIONS TO CONSIDER

1. How do you think Ernie Pyle's columns made people at home feel about the war effort?

2. What about the infantry appealed to Pyle?

3. How would you explain the different attitudes of soldiers toward Germans they are fighting and the ones they have taken prisoner?

Humor of
Bill Mauldin

After serving for a year in the infantry, Bill Mauldin went to work as a cartoonist for the military newspaper, Stars and Stripes. His cartoons were soon published in hundreds of newspapers in the United States as well, where he became the most widely read cartoonist of the war. Mauldin's cartoons were known both for their humor and their realistic portrayal of life at the front.

▲

At Pine Camp, New York, where temperatures got to thirty below, my work began to take on some form and relevance.

Pine Camp, N. Y.

▲

"That's all for this morning, men. Dismissed . . . I said DISMISSED!"

▲

"Don't ask foolish questions. Th' schedule calls
for calisthenics. We'll start with th' left eyelid."

▲

"Wisht I could stand up an' git some sleep."

"My, sir—what an enthusiastic welcome!"

"Hit th' dirt, boys!"

c2ca

▲

"How ya gonna find out if they're fresh troops if ya
don't wake 'em up an' ask?"

▲

" . . . forever, Amen. Hit the dirt!"

▲
"Just gimme th' aspirin. I already got a Purple Heart."

"Don't look at me, lady. I didn't do it."

War Diary

BY DESIDERIO J. SAIS

A regular soldier in the war, Desiderio J. Sais was a rancher from Albuquerque, New Mexico, before becoming Technician, 5th Grade in the army. He was in charge of trucks and the amphibious vehicles, known familiarly as Ducks, that carried troops across land and water. His diary records the last years of the war in Italy and Germany.

ITALY

February 2, 1944—Went in to some of the houses here, and they sure are badly damaged. Many still have fine furniture.

February 3—Wittenmaier brought me a spring bed. But I still can't sleep good at night. Could it be the noise?

February 4—Was in Motor Pool when air raid occurred. Jumped in small fox hole. Olson & Stewart beat me there, but I landed on top of both. All clear, not much damage done.

February 5—Received first *Stars & Stripes*. So now we can get an account of the war. We are still pushing forward, as also are the British.

February 6—It was very quiet last night. Whistling Willie (German gun) is still continuing to come over. One landed on the road. Did some damage.

February 7—Big air-raid. We knock down four planes. Saw one jump from plane.

February 8—Area hit by bomb lost kitchen tent & truck. C.O.[1] wounded. Many other things happened on that same day *(me hit also!!!)*

February 9—Received nice box of candy from Ursula and was enjoyed by all. It was kind of quiet today.

February 10—Got up and found most of our trucks damaged by a nite raid. Shields went to the hospital.

February 11—Today I received lots of mail. Glad to know that everyone at home are fine.

February 12—Received *Readers Digest* so am trying to occupy my mind by reading.

February 13—After so long a time I finally got a hair-cut by a G.I. I expect to take a bath soon, I hope.

February 14—Went to QM.[2] I found a pair of water boots. I jumped in another fox-hole. 18 of us in all, both black & white (G.I.)

February 15—Went to the Day Room to do some reading and catching up with my writing. Hq. moved in with us, so had to move to other cave.

February 17—Four air-raids last night. German mission was not accomplished. They lost four more planes.

---

[1] C.O.—commanding officer.
[2] QM—quarter master, the supply department.

February 18—A P-38 landed on area. The pilot was not injured as he bailed out in time.

February 19—Today was a big day for me cause I finally took a shower. The weather, I mean the water (the Whistling Willie is getting on me nerves) was nice & warm.

February 20—Keeping busy in area, I also did my own laundry. It took me long to finish as I was always on the run. Yes, for a fox-hole.

February 21—William & Freiburg went to hospital. Condition not serious. An air-raid is going on and I am here on my bed. My fingers crossed. Everything under control.

February 22—Received letter from Ray saying he sold calves at KC and also that he is moving.

February 23—Air-raid last night destroyed Ducks.

February 24—Don't feel too good, had only one meal. Whistling Willie is around again.

February 25—Today I feel better. No air-raids today. I washed, shaved, and did some more reading. A few more trucks were damaged.

February 26—Took trucks to front. Four got stuck. Pull them out before daylite.

February 27—Sgt. of guard again. Everything under control. Very little noise.

February 28—Took laundry, mine & Sgt. Elliott to an Italian lady. Gave her some C-rations. . . .

May 16—Left the 53 QM Trk Bn and landed in Naples. We are now attached to the 6723 Trk Group (Prov.) Co. We landed here the following day by an LST.[3]

---

[3] LST—ship that comes up to the shore or beach to load and unload troops (the initials stand for "landing ship troop").

May 17—Fixing up our new area. We are living in squad tents with eight men in it.

May 18—I haven't been to Naples yet. Expecting on going tomorrow. Rumors that limited service men will get to go to the States on points. Received my Purple Heart. The serial no. is 19711. Planning on sending it home. It rained today. It's a good thing because it sure has been dusty.

May 19—Went to Naples and then to Caivano. Had a nice time. Stayed most of the time at the Red Cross.

May 25, 1944—Moved again, this time we are attached to 6748 Co. C. Just 17 men were transferred.

May 26—Went to see Nina and took her my laundry. She had films for my camera. We took pictures.

May 27—Went to Naples. MPs[4] are on the ball. Many of our boys spend the nite in the Guard House. One boy didn't salute an officer (90 day wonder), others didn't have **dogtags**,[5] etc.

May 28—Took my laundry to Nina. She does a good job and doesn't charge me anything. I take her gum and cigarettes.

May 29—Rode LST to Anzio with load of French Ammo. Reported to assembly area of 6723 Co. C. trk.

June 2—Did some hauling. Also had a big night air-raid.

June 5—Haul German prisoners to the cemetery to dig graves. Took a shower at 5 Army Hq. Received new issue of clothing.

---

[4] MPs—MP stands for "military police."

[5] **dogtags**—metal identification tags that soldiers were supposed to wear at all times.

June 6—Took ammo to Rome. On the way saw many Germans (dead), "tanks," etc. People walking back to their homes that they left six months ago. Plenty of people in Rome to welcome us. Pretty buildings and beautiful girls. Yesterday was the first day for the GI's to enter Rome.

June 7—Haul rations to Rome. Stayed over night but didn't get a chance to see St. Peter's Cathedral.

June 8—Am assigned to Co. B 3338 QM Trk Co., stationed at Anzio. Cooper is also here.

June 9—Nice outfit. Haven't done much yet so am getting a good rest. Am expecting to go to Rome on a pass.

June 10—Didn't get a pass today. I drove a Duck today. Went after a load of rations from boat (Liberty). P.B.S. trying to get control of Rome. 5Th Army (Gen. Clark) still going strong. They are now 80 mi. beyond Rome. Received lots of mail today. Went to 6723 area and got Dave Malanut's dog (Butch). Rest of boys went to Replacement Center. Cooper, Elliott, Thompson & myself are assigned to the 53 (Duck Bn) Co. B in Anzio.

June 11—Went to Rome on pass with Cooper, saw St. Peter's Cathedral. Walked around town. Lots of people and G.I.s. Eat downtown. Meal wasn't so good.

June 12—Drive the Duck again, from ship (water) to the ration dump.

June 13—Went to our old area to take a shower but crew left for Rome. So we went in the beach. The water was nice but salty. Lots of GI's are swimming. Civilians are still coming thru, some going home, others to Rome and Naples.

June 14—Went to the Ration Dump to get the rations. Also went to "C" Co. area. Boys in dug-out found a house mate. People still traveling on the hi-way going home.

June 15—Went to Rome again. Saw the beautiful cathedral of St. Peter. Did a lot of sight-seeing. Met a girl, Agnes De Sintos. Invited us over to her house for lunch. Didn't have much but enjoyed it. She gave me her picture.

June 16—Saw Ed Chavez & Augustin Eichwald on their way to Rome. Here in Anzio getting rations for the 88th Div. 5th Army. Are now about 100 mi. No. of Rome. We are expecting to move soon. Now we are hauling from the docks with Ducks.

June 18—Rumors that we will finally get paid (last paid Oct.-9 mo.) My little dog (Butch) is OK and sure growing. Took him riding today. . . .

August 15—Invasion took place in S. France. A big success. We are getting along OK.

August 16—Arrive Staging Area.[6] French & English troops also here. Went to Naples & Bagnolia.

August 17—Went to Naples again. Many troops pulling out. The harbor is full of LST's.

August 18—Went to Bagnolia to see Nina & also to get the films I left there before I went to Anzio.

August 19—Still eating "C" rations. We are getting ready to leave. I think tomorrow we will be going to France.

August 20—Loading up on LST. Ruziski & I are on the same Duck & Butch is still with us.

---

[6] staging area—the place where troops or supplies are assembled before a military operation.

August 21—We are on our way. Smooth riding. Butch is getting plenty to eat from the sailors. We are eating "C" rations.

August 22—Saw some big fish. The water is getting rough.

August 23—Expecting to land today. We now can see land. We unloaded. Had trouble with the Duck but finally had it fixed. Was on land for about 8 hrs. Moved to our new area. Can't find Butch & "Anzio," so I reported them missing in action.

August 24—Reached our new area. We are now living in houses again. The nearest town is San Raphael. The buildings are not badly damaged. The French people here are kind & friendly. I am expecting to go to town after I finish packing.

August 25—Took a Duck to the docks to work, hauled rations & ammo. Took my laundry to Mr. Martinez. He's from Spain. Told me all about the Germans. Girls that went with them had their head shaved.

August 26—Went to town, San Raphael, to get a haircut. Vino cost 10 francs a glass (20 cents). Haul rations from Liberty ship. Polish prisoners working in Ration Dump. Before going to bed Snow, Brown & "Buck" & I cooked some bacon.

August 27—Raining plenty & I have to take my Duck out. The rest of the boys that were left in Naples arrived today. Hogan found himself a room mate. Wow!

August 28—Haven't found Butch yet but still looking for him. After work went to Antonio Martinez's house & had dinner (San Raphael). . . .

December 10-44—Left Camp La Bonne (school) with the Ducks. Slept in Beaune and arrived in our new area, Langres on 12-13-44. We are staying in a school house.

Hq. is eating with us. We unloaded our Ducks cause tomorrow we are suppose to turn them in. Langres is a small town.

December 14—We took our Ducks to Beaune. We are suppose to work in an ammo dump here in town. Arriving back to camp I heard the sad news that our Capt. Kelly was in an accident (Jeep turned over and froze to death). Tomorrow I am going to town and look for a shower.

December 23-44—Went to **confession**[7] at the Cathedral. No Army Chaplain but the Parish priest understands good English. Might go to Dijon for Xmas service.

December 24—Went to mass at the Cathedral. It was plenty cold. In fact the altar boys wore gloves. Many GI's attended. Tomorrow is Xmas & expecting a big dinner. Today I didn't work since my feet are giving me trouble.

December 25—Xmas day. Went to Mass & Holy Communion at the Cathedral here in Langres. Snowing & plenty cold. Played poker & knock rummy. Will work tonite.

December 26—We are now off days & work at nights at Ammo.

December 27—Having trouble with my feet. Made sick call. Don't work today. Tonite we will.

December 28—Just about finish moving ammo. Went to town & got hair-cut. Received a letter from Simone from Marseille & also photo. Wow!

December 29—Finish ammo. Tomorrow we will go to Marseille and bring new trucks to Langres.

---

[7] **confession**—act of telling sins to a priest and asking for forgiveness.

December 30–31—On our way to Marseille. We slept in Valence ate "C" rations and started next morning & arriving in the evening. Got a pass & went to see Feli. Family were surprise to see me. Had supper there. We slept in area "C." Kitchen went AWOL.[8]

January 1-45—Went after our new big trucks. Had dinner with a Port Bn. Tonite they will serve chicken. Got ready & went over to see Feli. Had supper with her and then went to the dance at Connet. Saw Stewart & Cooper & girl friends.

January 2—Took trucks to Ord. to be loaded didn't finish until about 10 at night. Suppose to go over to see Feli but didn't since it was late.

January 4—Finally arrived here in camp. With our trucks empty (unloaded at Dijon). Kitchen finally came back (AWOL). Haven't eaten or slept much so tonite will retire early.

January 5—We are now on the alert & can't leave area. I was planning on taking a bath. Getting ready to leave again & this time we are going the other direction. Gilbert is my assistant.

January 6—We are leaving again. Last night we slept at Epinal. It is snowing and the ground is plenty slippery. We arrived at our destination OK. The name of the town we're in is Strasbourg. We are ordered to leave the town as the Germans are expecting to take over. So we are now in Molsheim. Just a few miles from the front. Most of the trucks went out. Gilbert & I have to haul (Infantry to the front). The boys were green, just came from the states (Rainbow Division). When unloading truck they marched to the front without the tools & a few without their ammo. We stayed at the CP & had

---

[8] AWOL—absent without leave, suggesting that his friend, nick-named Kitchen, left the base without permission.

coffee & bread. 4 o'clock in the morning Sgt. Lewis came by & we all went back but got lost & didn't reach camp (Molsheim) until the next day.

January 7—We are now hauling German captured ammo to the rear. The people of Strasbourg all speak German. The beer is good here & a nice town but can't trust the people.

January 8—Hauling French ammo to railhead. Sanchez found a dead soldier (G.I.), loaded him in truck & took him to the nearest camp.

January 9—Doing the same thing. The town is very big & the people are undecided to be for Germans or Americans. In most houses you will see American & French flags one day & then the next day they will be down.,. . . .

March 15—Been traveling for the past two days. We are now in an area just a few miles from Nancy. We are living in tents. I believe we will train here and get ready for "the river crossing." Warm today, just like summer. Had no trouble on the road. We are 282 mi. from Lyon. There is a small village near by. Guess I will go in and get my laundry done. We are now with the 7th Army again.

March 18—Had a Duck inspection. We are getting ready to move. I think we will move close to Luneville or thereabouts. Dunlop & McGuire came back (AWOL) to area. Today it is cold.

March 19—Went to Nancy on a pass. Had a nice time. Took a shower & pictures to be developed.

March 22—Getting ready to move. I think we will go to Germany.

March 23—Got everything packed & on our way. We slept in a field and expecting to continue on our journey.

March 25—We are now in German soil. Many houses destroyed & people moving out. We are not allowed to speak to them. I guess from now on I will have to do my own laundry. Gilbert, Populaski & I rode on one Duck. It rained most of the way.

March 26—Put up a tent near a small town. It is Off Limited so can't go in. So I now find time to do some letter writing.

March 27—The 7th Army crossed the Rhine River. Don't know what we will do. Hauling ammo across the Rhine River at night. I got lost the first night but made it back to camp OK. Made two loads. Populaski is working with A-frame across the river.

March 28—I'm working nights. I cross the Rhine again. I have a good Duck. We can not talk to the people here. So when I get back I usually go to sleep. Many homes are destroyed. GI's are riding around in civilian cars & motor-cycles.

March 29—Still moving ammo. 7th Army are 75 mi. in now & connected with the 3rd Army. Ammo here about finished. The German soldiers left most of their equipment behind as they were in a hurry to leave.

March 30—Windy & still working nights hauling ammo to the front. For dinner today we all received one big bottle of German wine & champaign. It tasted pretty good. I went in a vacant house and manage to get a mattress, so now perhaps I will keep warm & sleep better. Many French civilians are on their way back to France (Labor).

April 1—I crossed the Rhine with lights on, but had a hard time getting to the other side. There was no one there to guide us in. I finally manage to find the entrance. We are expecting to move soon. A C D Cos. have already left.

April 2—We are now in Limberhof, arriving today. Hauling rations from Dump to Depot across the Rhine. Expecting to finish within the next few days. Many houses destroyed & people traveling along the road. We are not allowed to talk or associate with them yet.

April 3—We were paid in French money ($35.00).

April 4—Still working days. Today I washed my Duck. Hauling rations & gas. Have to do my own laundry today.

April 5—Haven't been feeling very well. I am driving nites.

April 6—Made sick-call. Have a fever of 102. Have malaria. Slept all day & taking treatment. May have to go to hospital if fever don't go down.

April 7—Feeling some better. Stayed in bed. Using Duck to haul ammo.

April 8—Feeling better, made sick call, still taking pills. Nice day. Boy from "C" Co. hit last night during air-raid. He died on way in.

April 9—Am up and feel better. Walked to the village with Pop & took some pictures. Ducks going out today.

April 10—Went out & haul some rations & gas across the river. White flags are still out. Nice night. One of the boys had trouble with Duck in water. Helped him get out.

April 11—Went out again. Had an air raid. Six boys got transfer today including Gilbert.

April 12—Feel good today. Received a package with carne seco & slippers from Mother.

April 13—Rumors that President Roosevelt died last night. Yes, it is true. He dies at Wash.

April 14—Went back to camp. Read my mail. Most of the other drivers are out.

April 18—Moved from Limberhof to another area. Haul 44 Division to the front, got scraped but no one was hurt. Arrived at night, chased civilians out & slept in house. Captured many prisoners. Found a radio, not much good.

April 21—Took the 103 Div. to the front. Had no chow, traveled all day & night. Came back for another load.

April 25—Took the 101 Airborne to new area. Haven't been feeling very well, driving both days & nights. My assistant can't drive nights.

April 26—Went back to the camp, and made sick call. Had a fever of 104. Went to the hospital. (112) Have malaria. Logan also went.

April 27—Spend one week in hospital and then went to the 2nd Con. for sev. days. Landed in the 71st Replacement Depot near Munich. Chow was *terrible*. Stayed here for three weeks, near the town where the S.S. troops starved the French & Russian slave workers. Many were found in box cars. Found a new bicycle. Did a lot of riding. Dachau, Weniger & I went out & found two rifles. Send them home. Manage to get plenty of eggs & beer. Refugees are doing a lot of looting, cars, etc. Nice weather just like summer.

May 1945—Played poker, lost a little. We have Russians working in the kitchen. Our meals are getting better. Trying to get out but no luck. Even wrote to the C.O.

May 8—The war here is officially finished! Went bicycle riding & also visited the concentration camp where the refugees are staying (French, Russians & Polish). We are staying in tents. The weather is nice & so are the girls but we can't fraternize. About everyone here in Germany have a bicycle. Had PX & finally got some cig. Haven't seen a stage show since I been over here. Went to the show. . . .

Left Antwerp Belgium Aug 26-45 Arrived Camp Kilmer, N.J. Sept. 8-45 Discharged Fort Bliss, Tex Sept. 1945 Civilian again! Wow!

QUESTIONS TO CONSIDER

1. What did you find most surprising about Sais's diary?

2. How would you describe his living conditions?

3. What does Sais's diary tell about the conditions of the people who lived in the war-torn countries he passed through?

4. What emotions can you infer from his diary?

Life in a German POW Camp

BY MICHAEL MAZZA

Michael Mazza was a 19-year-old infantry rifleman from Massachusetts when he was captured. He had been wounded, and first went to a hospital in Hoenstein, Germany. Then he was sent to a POW (prisoner of war) camp. In this part of his diary, he tells about his time in the camp until the end of the war.

August 6, 1944—There were about 3000 other Americans at this camp waiting to be sent out to different work camps. I was called for examination on the 25th of June by the camp doctor. He gave me a slip of paper stating that I was only able to do light work. But I was still to be sent out to a farm to work. Our camp spokesman was trying until 9:30 at night to get me off of the work list but it was to no avail. I was to leave on the 28th for a farm in Rowen, Germany, with three other Yanks.[1]

---

[1] Yanks—short for Yankee; someone from the United States.

We left at 6 A.M. and slept in a barn in Lauenburg that night. We reached our destination the next day around noon. It was a small shack attached to a pigpen. There were 20 other Americans at the farm and they were all glad to see new faces. We stayed up until late that night getting the **low down**[2] on what to expect and getting acquainted with one another. They were taken prisoner about six months before we were in Africa. Everyone has their own details to take care of in the barracks. There was one guy who was the chef and he knew how to cook potatoes about 15 different ways, which made it better when you had to eat them every day. I guess I was starting to get used to everything because even the German black bread started to taste like bread.

I started out doing light work but the Kraut[3] boss I had didn't like the idea because it wasn't long before I was out working along side of the other men. We worked right with the German men and women civilians. There were a few Russian girls who, I imagine, were prisoners also. The days seemed to pass pretty fast while working in the fields. But the nights, when one had time to think, seemed to drag by. Before the lights went out at 10 P.M. we played chess, checkers, or cards to pass the time away.

American bombers flew over today. The first I've seen since I left the hospital. They dropped empty auxiliary gas tanks in Rowen and their bombs about 30 or 40 miles from here. The rumbling could be heard off in the distance.

August 15—I guess the Russians must be making quite a bit of headway because the Krauts are sending civilians and P.O.W.'s up to East Prussia to build trenches

---

[2] **low down**—real facts, truth.

[3] Kraut—often during wartime soldiers use negative nicknames for their enemies, as shown here when the soldiers refer to the Germans as "Krauts."

for the retreating soldiers. Some of the women, who work practically as hard as the horses, also went along. We've been pretty fortunate so far, none of us have been selected to go.

August 31—I received my first letter from the States today, dated July 4th, from my brother and his wife. This is my first news from home since November in '43 when I left home for overseas.

September 7—The German inspector came around today to look over the horses. Twelve are being taken away to be eaten by the soldiers at the front to keep them going. They will probably tell them it is prime beef. Last week they rounded up all the dogs in the neighborhood. What next!

September 8—I felt kind of sick for the last couple of days so I'm not working today. The guard had some pills sent from the doctor in the next town. I hope they do some good.

September 9—Well, I finally got a couple of letters from home. I feel a lot better today so I got out of bed. My fever has gone down some so I'll probably be back to work Monday.

September 10—I had a good breakfast today. I traded some cigarettes for a couple of eggs and had spam and eggs. They really hit the spot. Well, with today being Sunday, it's washday again. Then after I get my haircut I'll take it easy for the rest of the day because we start digging potatoes tomorrow. It will take quite a while to get them all dug because that is practically all that is planted here.

September 28—Mail has seemed to slow down again. It's been a couple of weeks since the last letter from home. Right now, with the Yanks in Germany, I don't think it will be too long before we will be heading for home.

Tomorrow will make three weeks that we have been picking potatoes with about two more to go.

October 4—Well, here it is (mittag) middle of the day and another five hours of work to go. With 2 $1/2$ more days to go before we get our Red Cross boxes, all I have left is a little coffee and some powdered milk. One of the boys gave me five packs of cigarettes to hold me until a package arrives from home.

November 2—I've been in bed with a cold for the past few days and I'm feeling pretty low. To top it off we got the news that starting next week we were going to be cut down from one Red Cross box a week to one every two weeks. I still haven't received a package from home but I hope they start coming soon. According to the letters I have received there are about a half dozen on the way.

November 18—My first package finally arrived today. It was filled with stuff, that I hadn't seen since leaving the states. Boy, what a banquet there will be tomorrow (Sunday) after I get my washing done. I don't think there will be anything left for the next day.

November 21—This is what you might call a red letter day. I got 10 letters in the mail today with news of more packages on the way. A few snapshots of the family and friends will also be enclosed. The packages will come in handy with only half of a Red Cross box a week being given us. It gets pretty tiresome eating potatoes three times a day seven days a week. I traded a couple of packs of butts for a chicken yesterday. When I cut it open it looked as though the chicken has some kind of a disease. So I was out a chicken and two packs of butts.

November 30—"Thanksgiving" but just another working day here. We had a wonderful dinner of potatoes, black bread, and that lousy German coffee. Well, I shouldn't complain, at least I'm still alive and able to eat. We have been getting quite a bit of rumors to the effect that we will be leaving here soon because the Reds[4] were making a big drive. The Germans want to get us to the American lines to be liberated rather than let the Reds retake us.

December 5—Well, here it is another day, and another 25 cents earned. I also got another letter from home today letting me know that everyone was well and feeling fine. I had a piece of goose today and I expect to have pork chops tomorrow night if the deal goes through. You can get something good to eat once in a while if you have any spare cigarettes to trade.

I hope a cigarette package comes from home soon so that I can trade for some chicken for my Christmas dinner. I'm beginning to wonder if the Krauts are grabbing them for themselves.

December 25—Christmas Day—This is my second Christmas away from home but I've managed to have turkey each time although it doesn't taste the same. The turkey came in cans out of our Red Cross boxes which arrived in the nick of time for the holidays. It was quite welcome to see them because we expected nothing at all.

January 28, 1945—Well, it's been a year and six days since I was taken prisoner and I honestly believe that in a couple of months I will be on my way out of here. It snowed all day yesterday and we had to work inside. With but little that can be done inside, we had it fairly easy. We have a five week supply of Red Cross boxes on hand now with rumors of more on the way.

---

[4] Reds—the Soviet forces or Russians.

February 11—I had to work on the straw detail today because of wet grounds. Eight wagons of refugees came into Rowen yesterday from East Prussia and about 80 ditch diggers. The Reds must be getting pretty close.

February 14—We have been cut down to half rations again so I guess I'll lose a little more weight. We are beginning to hurt as much as the Germans now with but little to eat. Four 'Limeys'[5] on their way to another Commando stopped overnight at our barracks. They said that with the Reds on one side and the Yanks on the other that we are practically cut off. That means that our rations are going to be cut down to the bone.

I earned about 14 marks last month. That's about $5.60 in American money. I hauled and delivered cabbage this afternoon and picked up three lard sandwiches from the civilians. I helped uncover two wagon-loads of spuds this morning.

February 16—I picked cow beets this morning and worked in the woods this afternoon. It was a cool and quiet day all around. I just can't wait for that half of a Red Cross box we get tomorrow so I can have something besides black bread and potatoes.

February 18—Well, it has finally come. We got word today that the Reds were making a big drive and that we were going to leave here tomorrow morning with everything that we own. We will go by wagon to a town not far from here.

March 10—We have now been on the road almost three weeks and are in Stolp, about 500 miles from where we started. We traveled about 250 miles the first week we were out and it was pretty rough. We started out with all our clothes and four Red Cross boxes each. By the time we had gone about ten miles, everything we had seemed as though they weighed twice as much.

---

[5] Limeys—the British.

We discarded most of the things that we figured were not going to be needed. Blankets, extra pants, shirts, canned powdered milk, and margarine. Later on we wished we were able to carry all the things we got rid of. There were about a thousand Frenchmen behind us in the march that were making good use of the stuff. At present the bread and oleo that we get for rations each day is what I am living on.

March 24—Here it is over a month now and still no idea where we are headed. We were issued one Red Cross box for every nine men which gave us about a bite apiece. We marched about 25 miles yesterday; so, for a change, they gave us today off. Except for one night when we slept out in the rain, we have been sleeping in barns. It was used for the sheep during the day and we used them at night.

March 29—We are now in Eversdorf, Germany. We are resting today but only because it is raining. Three days ago we received three Red Cross boxes for every five men. It didn't go very far, but it sure helped. All these Krauts are giving us is a piece of bread and potato soup once a day. I will be able to picture the wonderful dinner they will be having at home next Sunday (Easter).

There was a bombing raid three days ago not far from where we stayed and those American planes really looked good. They are over this section of the country almost every day now. We walked through Salswedel yesterday and it looked as if it had been hit just recently.

My ankles have been bothering me quite a bit lately and I have developed a few blisters on my feet, but my hopes are high and I think I'll make it to the end. Wherever that is?

April 1—Easter Sunday 7:30 A.M. I am in Messdorf, what part of Germany that is in I don't know. Right now it is cloudy and windy so I guess today will probably be another wet one. I imagine the planes will be over again today but we won't be able to see them.

One of the boys managed to get a couple of buckets of spuds,[6] so guess we will have enough of something to fill our stomachs. I imagine the Krauts will put on quite a hunt for them but as usual they won't turn up.

Today marks the sixth week we have been on the march with no knowledge of where we are headed for. ·

April 3—We are now six kilometers from Stendal. My buddy confiscated three dozen of eggs yesterday and while we were boiling them we had them covered with potatoes so that the Krauts wouldn't spot them. When they found out they were missing and started to look for them, they looked everywhere but under the spuds. And only yesterday morning they found out that about 400 pounds of spuds were missing. We will be here about six days so I guess that a lot of other things will be missing before we leave.

April 11—About 400 people were killed in a big bombing raid in Stendal, the place we left a couple of days ago. We are now in a pretty good-sized town called Tangermunde. We walked about 18 kilometers[7] and my ankles are all swelled up so that I can hardly stand. We heard a rumor to the effect that starting tomorrow we are going to be working on the railroads. Our rations are getting so that it's just about enough to keep us going. We have been out of Red Cross boxes for so long that I am beginning to forget how good food is beginning to taste.

April 12—We are supposed to leave here this morning but rumors are flying again. They say that the Yanks are making a big drive toward Tangermunde and that we are unable to move on. Boy, I sure hope so. We had

---

[6] spuds—potatoes.
[7] 18 kilometers—11.18 miles.

our soup around noon and are waiting for word to move out. About 12:17 a shell landed close to the building we are staying in and we all headed for cover. The Americans had finally reached us. They kept up with the artillery, laying it in pretty heavy until about 3:30 and then everything got quiet. About 6:30 an American officer and a private came walking into the yard. The German captain immediately handed over his surrender papers, which he had been holding in his hand since the barrage started, to the American officer. Believe me, it was the happiest moment of my life. As we marched out we could see American soldiers everywhere. We got a few rations from the food trucks and ate them as though we had never eaten before. The white bread looked and tasted like sponge cake compared to what we had been eating.

The Yanks told us that President Roosevelt had died that day. It was such a shock that none of us believed it at first.

April 14—They loaded us on trucks and took us to a town about 20 miles from here. While on the way we were strafed by German fighter planes and we had to stop and scatter. Luckily no one was shot. When we reached the town the people were good enough to move out and let us use their homes. For a late snack that night we had fried chicken, french fried potatoes, and a little wine to wash it down.

April 20—We were loaded onto trucks this morning and headed out to the air field. We boarded a plane and were off to France. This was my first plane ride. It took us about four hours to get here and when we arrived we were greeted by Red Cross workers with hot coffee and doughnuts. Real American coffee. We then boarded trucks at the field and went out to Camp Lucky Strike. After a good **delousing**[8] and a change of clothes we all

---

[8] **delousing**—washing with chemicals to remove lice.

got ready to go out and do the town. But as we were all restricted we could not leave the camp at all.

About a week later the boat docked and we were loaded on. We reached port in Virginia and immediately went out to Camp Patrick Henry. We were marched in to a movie to listen to a talk from some officer. He said that we would have all the time we were there to ourselves but that we couldn't leave the camp. Then came our first meal back in the States. It was one of the best meals that I ever had or will ever have in the Army. Maybe it was because I hadn't had steak for so long, but it still tasted better than I've ever had before.

After about a week of knocking around, the guys from the New England area were shipped to Fort Devens. When we reached there we were immediately given a physical. They said that in a couple of days we would be going home and that when we returned we would be sent to some resort for recuperation. But, to my disappointment, I had to report to the hospital for a rest because I was suffering from malnutrition. I was only 30 miles from home now and I still couldn't get there. I sent a telegram telling them that I had arrived and that I couldn't get home right away. That Sunday, Mother's Day, practically the whole family came up to see me. I was asleep when they arrived and they were standing around the bed waiting for me to wake up. I guess they didn't want to disturb me. When I finally was awakened I was a much surprised man. After being away for so long they all seemed to be strangers to me. Boy, what a feeling you get when you look at your own parents and don't recognize them. After talking for a while though, everything came back to me. After bringing me up to date on all the news, I felt like one of the family again.

QUESTIONS TO CONSIDER

1. What do you think of the German treatment of prisoners of war, based on this account?

2. Why were prisoners moved so much? What was happening in the war that would explain it?

3. Being bombed by Americans seems to please rather than worry Mazza. How would you explain his reaction?

War in the Pacific

The Bombing of Pearl Harbor: A Nurse's Eyewitness Account

BY MYRTLE WATSON

On December 7, 1941, the Japanese attacked the U.S. Pacific Fleet at its base in Pearl Harbor, Hawaii. This act led the United States to enter World War II. All Americans old enough to understand could tell you exactly what they were doing when they first heard about the Japanese attack on the naval base at Pearl Harbor. The first bombs that fell on Oahu landed near the Schofield Barracks. Myrtle Watson, an army nurse on duty that morning, tells of the air strike.

On that Sunday morning, I was working on the orthopedic ward with only a few other nurses. We were busy after breakfast wheeling bedridden men onto the second-story porch so that they could watch a barefoot football game about to begin. I remember it was about

7:45 A.M. As we stood on the porch looking out at the field, we heard the low sound of planes coming overhead. Some people on the ground and the porch began waving at the planes. Our curiosity was aroused because the planes just kept coming. There was no letup.

I was standing in the doorway looking at the planes with an injured GI named Jack. Jack, who called me Chick because of my blond hair, seemed to have a crush on me and followed me around like a shadow. We couldn't quite recognize the planes, and I said to Jack that I didn't think they were our planes. Jack, who was a sergeant and knew planes, said, "Chick, I think we're at war." I said in a rather shaky voice, "We couldn't be at war; someone would tell us." We just stood frozen in our places staring at the sky as the planes made their runs. The effect was almost **hypnotic**.[1]

When we recognized the rising-sun insignia and heard the explosions start to go off, we pushed the beds back into the ward so that they would be under cover. When I went back onto the porch to wheel in the second group of men, the planes were flying so low you could see the goggles and scarves on the pilots. The sound of gunfire and the drone of the plane engines intensified. Jack was still out on the porch and I was standing next to him when suddenly he shoved me aside and to the floor of the porch. A line of bullets was cutting a path from the ground and up the side of the building. Two heavy bullets lodged in the door frame, right where my knees would have been. Just a fraction of a second longer, and the strafing[2] would have cut me off at the knees. I almost became a patient in my own ward. I got up trembling all over and headed for the safety of the ward. I felt a little foolish when I thought of the ideal

---

[1] **hypnotic**—having the effect of putting one into a trance.
[2] strafing—machine-gun fire from a low-flying airplane.

target that I presented to the diving planes. The only thing I lost in the ordeal was my nurse's cap.

After I got back inside the ward, I began cutting some of the guys out of **traction**[3] and moving them under their beds. As the strafing was still going on, I piled mattresses around them, then climbed under the bed with them.

Within minutes of the attack, the wounded started to stream in the hospital. For three days, there seemed to be an inexhaustible supply of wounded and dying men. They were bringing men in so quickly that they didn't have time to separate the living from the dead. Bodies were piling up like **cordwood**[4] wherever there was space. It was unbelievable what I was seeing. Some men were missing arms and legs, while others had limbs hanging by a shred of skin. It was hard to think that these men might be considered lucky since they had an outside chance of pulling through. The saddest and most depressing cases were the burn victims. Some of the men that were brought in were charred to a crisp, while others had their skin burned off, so their bodies resembled strips of fried and partially burnt bacon. It amazed the medical staff that these men were still alive when they were brought in.

Until the doctors had a chance to examine the more severely injured and wounded men, the nurses did their best to comfort them and see to their immediate needs. We were constantly changing dressings and checking vital signs. Basins were placed beneath the beds to catch the blood that soaked through the thin hospital mattresses. Empty whiskey and vodka bottles filled with hot water served as hot-water bottles to men in shock. The first man who died on me was a young, dark and handsome nineteen-year old sergeant. When he came to

---

[3] **traction**—the medical equipment used to create a pulling force that helps heal broken bones.

[4] **cordwood**—stacked piles of cut firewood.

the ward, he was minus two legs and suffering from abdominal wounds. There was another young fellow I was helping who looked up at me, saw my nail polish, and said, "Nail polish . . . on an officer . . . in the middle of a war." Two hours later, he was dead.

The next three days following the attack were a blur of activity: nursing the dying, giving them whiskey and morphine,[5] eating only chocolate bars and coffee, worrying about a Japanese invasion, little sleep, blood, death, and more blood. Red became the prevailing color as blood seemed to work its way into every nook and cranny of the hospital. Although it meant very little to the wounded men at the time, they were fortunate that the island had fully staffed and well-equipped medical facilities. If they had been elsewhere in the Pacific, it is doubtful that many of them would have survived. We were prepared for almost any type of emergency, short of an all-out attack on the island. Despite the suddenness of the attack, the only items we ran low on were blood and space. The shortage of blood was only temporary. Once the call went out for donors, we had hundreds of men lining up to give blood for their comrades and buddies who had just spilled their own. The lack of space was something we had to learn to live with. Until arrangements could be made to move some of the men to other buildings, hallways had to serve as temporary wards.

I think what hurt and stuck with many of us who cared for the wounded was the fact that these young fellows were so spirited and so young and had no chance to protect themselves. It didn't seem fair that these fellows didn't have a fighting chance. Many of the soldiers at Schofield Barracks had gone to bed numb with Saturday night parties and awoke to an alarm clock of bombs and bullets, signaling the end of something and

---

[5] morphine—a pain killer.

the beginning of something else. When you picture young men going off to war, you hear bands and you see marching and flags waving. These poor guys had been awakened suddenly. They were hobbling out, trying to get on their packs, pulling up their zippers, and adjusting helmets. It made you wonder what kind of chance they could have. As the men scurried around the base trying to find their units or battle stations, you could see the smoke from Pearl Harbor in the background. It was not an encouraging sight for those who did not know what was happening in the harbor below us.

QUESTIONS TO CONSIDER

1. What led Watson to realize the planes were Japanese and that an attack was beginning?

2. What were conditions like in the hospital after the attack?

3. How did people respond? How do you think you might have responded?

4. What does Watson mean when she says that the bombs and bullets "signal the end of something and the beginning of something else" for the soldiers at Schofield Barracks?

Homefront

▲

Couponing Customers used coupon books to buy their allotted
share of scarce items.

Rationing Many goods such as shoes and gasoline were in short supply during the war, so people often stood in rationing lines.

Victory Gardens Citizens often planted small plots of vegetables during the war to provide some of the food that was in short supply. Called Victory Gardens, these street corner plots also added to the social life of the times.

▼

"We're just *made* for each other... I water his victory garden, and he stakes my tomato plants."

Rosie the Riveter During the war, women took jobs in factories to aid the war effort. The image of women had begun to change dramatically with their new role in the workforce, now that they had shown they could be as productive as men.

Morale Posters stressed the common war the U.S. was fighting at home and abroad. They emphasized the need for maintaining high morale and for making sacrifices for the common good.
▼

◀ **Civil rights denied** On February 19, 1942, President Franklin Roosevelt signed Executive Order 9066 which authorized the Department of War to designate military areas in the United States and exclude any or all persons from this area. As part of this order, Japanese-Americans were ordered to report to the War Relocation Authority. From there they were evacuated from the West Coast to inland internment camps, where they lived for the duration of the war.

Order No. 20 Under Civilian Exclusion Order No. 20, Japanese were told to report to Relocation centers where they were "processed" and transported to internment camps.

▼

▲
FDR President Roosevelt addressed the nation many times during the war. His speeches became justly famous for the strength they inspired and his occasionally witty humor.

Declaring War (Upper Right) Here President Roosevelt signs the declaration of war he asked for immediately after the bombing of Pearl Harbor.

A Date Which Will Live in Infamy

BY PRESIDENT FRANKLIN D. ROOSEVELT

In his speech to Congress the morning after Pearl Harbor was bombed, President Franklin Roosevelt declared December 7, 1941, "a date which will live in infamy." Here is that speech.

Yesterday, December 7, 1941—a date which will live in infamy[1]—the United States of America was suddenly and deliberately attacked by naval and air forces of the Empire of Japan.

The United States was at peace with that nation and, at the solicitation of Japan, was still in conversation with its Government and its Emperor looking toward the maintenance of peace in the Pacific. Indeed, one hour after Japanese air squadrons had commenced bombing in Oahu, the Japanese Ambassador to the United States and his colleague delivered to the Secretary of State a

---

[1] live in infamy—forever be known for its evil.

formal reply to a recent American message. While this reply stated that it seemed useless to continue the existing diplomatic negotiations, it contained no threat or hint of war or armed attack.

It will be recorded that the distance of Hawaii from Japan makes it obvious that the attack was deliberately planned many days or even weeks ago. During the intervening time the Japanese Government has deliberately sought to deceive the United States by false statements and expressions of hope for continued peace.

The attack yesterday on the Hawaiian Islands has caused severe damage to American naval and military forces. Very many American lives have been lost. In addition American ships have been reported torpedoed on the high seas between San Francisco and Honolulu.

Yesterday the Japanese Government also launched an attack against Malaya. Last night Japanese forces attacked Hong Kong. Last night Japanese forces attacked Guam. Last night Japanese forces attacked the Philippine Islands. Last night the Japanese attacked Wake Island. This morning the Japanese attacked Midway Island.

Japan has, therefore, undertaken a surprise offensive extending throughout the Pacific area. The facts of yesterday speak for themselves. The people of the United States have already formed their opinions and well understand the implications to the very life and safety of our nation.

As Commander-in-Chief of the Army and Navy, I have directed that all measures be taken for our defense.

Always will we remember the character of the onslaught against us.

No matter how long it may take us to overcome this **premeditated**[2] invasion, the American people in their righteous might will win through to absolute victory.

---

[2] **premeditated**—planned in advance.

I believe I interpret the will of the Congress and of the people when I assert that we will not only defend ourselves to the uttermost but will make very certain that this form of treachery shall never endanger us again.

Hostilities exist. There is no blinking at the fact that our people, our territory and our interests are in grave danger.

With confidence in our armed forces—with the unbounded determination of our people—we will gain the inevitable triumph—so help us God.

I ask that the Congress declare that since the unprovoked and **dastardly**[3] attack by Japan on Sunday, December seventh, a state of war has existed between the United States and the Japanese Empire.

---

[3] **dastardly**—sneaky, malicious, and cowardly.

QUESTIONS TO CONSIDER

1. Compare the words that Roosevelt used to describe the Japanese invaders with the words he used to describe the American people. What is the effect of each on the listener or reader?

2. How would you have responded to this message from the President?

3. Because the United States had earlier cracked the Japanese military codes, they had known that a large attack was being planned. How do you think that knowledge affected the peace negotiations Roosevelt describes?

Life in the Internment Camps

BY RICHARD LIDZ

The internment camps for the Japanese Americans were in isolated parts of Arizona, California, Colorado, Idaho, Utah, and Wyoming. They were built hurriedly without adequate supplies. They were surrounded by barbed wire and guarded by armed soldiers. In the book Many Kinds of Courage: An Oral History of World War II, *author Richard Lidz presents interviews with two prisoners who lived in the internment camps.*

Despite the discrimination they suffered before and during the war, most Japanese Americans displayed unfailing loyalty to the United States. There was not a single incident of sabotage. On the contrary, Nisei[1] with particular language skills were recruited for military intelligence work. On the day the army announced that they would accept Nisei volunteers, more than 1,200 signed up.

---

[1] Nisei—the people born in the United States of Japanese parents. Nisei are American citizens.

Before the war was over nearly 18,000 had joined the Army. No Nisei ever deserted. In Italy the famed 442nd Infantry, made up entirely of Nisei, lost three times its original strength, and was awarded 3,000 Purple Hearts with 500 oak leaf clusters,[2] 810 Bronze Stars, 342 Silver Stars, 47 Distinguished Service Crosses, and 17 Legion of Merit awards. Bill Mauldin wrote of the 442nd that "no combat unit in the Army could exceed them in loyalty, hard work, courage, and sacrifice . . . their casualty rates were appalling." Yet, when a Nisei who had lost a leg in Italy visited San Francisco during the war, he was beaten.

It was not until after the war, when people's attitudes had begun to change, that the Alien Land Act was declared **unconstitutional**[3] and the law preventing Orientals from becoming naturalized citizens was removed. But these official acts of conciliation[4] could not erase the experience of internment from the memories of those who had lived through it.

James Kazato, who had come to the United States in 1919, was one of the first 600 Japanese-Americans taken into custody. He was held in a detention camp for enemy **aliens**.[5] Roy Yano came here with his parents in 1917. He was sent to what the government euphemistically called a "relocation center." To the people who were forced to live in them, these relocation centers were America's concentration camps.

James Kazato:

When the war broke out, all of us were really shocked. But what shocked us—what shocked me most—was that all of us, regardless of whether we had American

---

[2] Purple Heart with oak leaf cluster—military personnel injured in action are awarded Purple Hearts. Oak leaf clusters represent multiple Purple Hearts, which go to people who return to action and are again injured.

[3] **unconstitutional**—illegal, against the U.S. constitution.

[4] acts of conciliation—efforts to regain goodwill.

[5] **aliens**—citizens of other countries.

citizenship or not, were put into concentration camps. If they had taken just the noncitizens, then it would have been all right. But I say to myself, why do they have to take all the American citizens? Because I knew that those born in the country, regardless of color, were American citizens. At that time Japan and Germany and the Italians were allies. Now I say to myself, well, if they are to take Japanese people, why not the Italians and Germans, too? That was my big question.

We were given very short notice. The government gave us just about ten days to pack and leave. I didn't have American citizenship. I wasn't given that chance— to be naturalized. So, as far as I'm concerned it was all right. But for my wife—she was an American citizen, and so are both my daughters, who were born here in San Francisco.

The government did not guarantee whether we could come back or not. They didn't promise us anything. So I told my wife, perhaps the good thing would be to sell our furniture and with that buy a bit of food and medicine and things like that. Since our younger daughter was only four months old and the older one was four years old, and we didn't know if there was doctors or hospitals in the camp, we took in as much medicine and baby food as possible.

Of course, I did have a number of nice friends. They came and gave us moral support, you might say. But at the same time there were a group of vultures who came in knowing that we had to leave. They came to buy our furniture in a way that was almost giving it away. They try to buy off your furniture for 50 cents or a dollar, something like that. We had this brand-new **mangle**.[6] Now we had two children, and I thought it would be nice if my wife can use that mangle for her ironing work. So we bought this brand new mangle about a month before this. It was still new, we used it only a few

---

[6] **mangle**—a machine for pressing sheets, and table linen.

times. And this man said he'd give us ten dollars. I said—by that time I got kind of mad—I said, "I would rather give it to someone who would just say thank you. Why should I give you for ten dollars?" So he said, "Well, I give you fifty dollars." By that time I was so mad, I said, "Get out!" I told him I'd sooner give it away free to anyone who would appreciate it and say thank you. But I don't want his dirty money. So I just kick him out.

We were sent to Topaz, Utah. That is about 200 miles directly south of Salt Lake City. I think there were close to 9,000 people in the camp, mostly from San Francisco. The living conditions were quite different from our home. Topaz was one mile square and within that there were 42 blocks. Each block consisted of barracks. Each barracks had about six rooms. And each family lived in one single room. Of course, if a party had a large family, actually he was given a larger room. Whereas a single man or a couple with no children were given a much smaller room. There were four of us.

My room was, I would say, 12 by 12 feet. Well, of course, there were just beds there, a small table, and a small bench—that was about it.

Now out of each twelve barracks, one was for dining and one was set aside for the shower rooms. So we had to eat out every time. We go to dining room where we had to line up. That's where we had our breakfast, lunch, and dinner.

When we first went to the camp, these barracks were built in such a hurry that there was no paved road or anything like that. It was just full of dust. It was built in the desert—every time we walked, all that powder would fly up, and from top to bottom we were covered with that white powder. And inside our room, too—no matter how many times you dust off, in a half hour the inside was full of dust. Eventually they watered the places, and later on they put a little oil on the dust so it wasn't too bad—say, maybe about a year or two later.

All the work was done by Japanese people who volunteered. Those who worked were paid. Like myself—I wanted to do something else other than barbering. But since I was a barber, most of my friends from San Francisco asked me that I should keep on as a barber. So I did, together with other barbers from other places. We were given $12 a month, but using our tools and all that, we thought that wasn't enough, so we asked for a little raise. So we got $16. I think those professional people, like doctors, were given $18. Naturally, with what little money we were given in those days, I bought whatever I can for the children. We were able to get out of the camp—not all of us. A few people represented the blocks, and they were asked to go and buy a few things.

The first thing we did in the camp, we built our churches. The Buddhist people got together and built their Buddhist church, and the Christian people built their own church. The older Nisei, who were out of college or high school, started teaching the children, and we set up schools.

Pretty soon the young people started playing baseball, and this and that, and it was just like outside. Older high school children had baseball games with outside teams. Like Caucasian people—we invited them to have a game with us.

To me the worst thing I experienced in the camp was that we didn't have privacy. For instance, each barracks had six families. And each was given one room, whether large or small. The barracks was built in such a way that there was a wide-open ceiling. So what happens is, when someone at the end would light up, the whole barracks would light up. And people with teenagers— what would happen in one room with a father and a mother and these children in the same room? If it's an overnight trip or something, it's all right. But we stayed there three and a half years.

When a person cannot have privacy, that is really bad. For myself, my children were young—it didn't matter too much. But I felt sorry for the people with teenage children. I remember when we got into the camp that a lot of bread and vegetables were carted in with cardboard boxes and things like that. You ought to see those people go after those cardboard boxes. We used them to make partitions, so as to make a little privacy. A lot of us had to adjust, but living under those conditions didn't do too good for the young people.

The mood of the Japanese changed considerably in those times. They adjusted themselves, knowing that they won't be able to get out. Of course, we were told that if we would like to get out voluntarily to outside of the camp, we were able to—other than to the Pacific Coast or Atlantic Coast. I don't know about the other people but, as far as I'm concerned, my children were still small and I thought staying in the camp was better for me simply because of the rumors. So, naturally, I wanted my family to stay because we knew that being in the camp we would be safe.

When the war was over I was very happy. But still we had to stay in the camp. But later on we were told that we can go back to California. By that time my land-lord, an Italian fellow—he was a very nice man—he kept this barber shop for me. During the wartime, all these three and a half years, he pulled the shades down and he just waited for me. And when he heard that we were able to come back to California, I had a letter from him saying, "Well, James, your shop is ready for you to open up, so you gotta come back." And I was really happy about it.

After we came back I would say I was one of the very few fortunate ones. Here I had my shop already waiting for me, and I was one of the very first ones to come back. I opened up and there were hardly any Japanese barbers then, so it kept me awfully busy.

Roy Yano:

When the war broke out in 1941 I was in Texas. It happened all of a sudden. I remember I heard the news on the radio and was totally surprised. I didn't expect anything like it to happen between Japan and America. The FBI picked me up that same night and put me in jail. I didn't know why, and they explained to me that I was an enemy alien. At that time Japanese people who were born in Japan were ineligible to become United States citizens. So when the war started we were enemy aliens.

They didn't apologize for picking me up and putting me in jail. They explained that since the war had started between the two countries it was their duty to put us in jail. We didn't argue. There were some Italians and Germans in the same jail. First we stayed in a city jail in Texas, then they sent us to a military establishment in San Antonio. Conditions weren't so bad because we didn't stay there too long. Then they established some kind of concentration camps for enemy aliens, not only Japanese, but Italians and Germans as well. So they sent us to Lordsburg, New Mexico, where there was a detention camp. At that time I was not married yet, I was single.

I had friends who came from Japan and worked for the Japanese Consulate or the foreign trade information office. They had to go back because they were sent from Japan especially for the job. I worked for the foreign trade office too, but I had a choice to stay here or go back because I had the status of permanent resident of the United States. I chose to stay here.

As an ineligible alien I was a Japanese subject. So when the war came, naturally I was considered an enemy alien and was sent to a regular concentration camp. We were sent to the camp in New Mexico in Army transport vehicles. When I was picked up, some of my American friends telephoned me, and others gave me notes of sympathy and so on, but not many of them came to help me because there wasn't much they could do. My car and all the personal property in my apartment were **confiscated**[7] by the government and stored in a government warehouse.

At the camp in New Mexico we had about five thousand Japanese people from all over the United States—Hawaii, Alaska, Texas, New York—but mostly from the Pacific Coast. And we lived in barracks under the control of the U. S. Army. There wasn't much furniture in the barracks. We had a bed, a couple of chairs and tables to write letters, and a mess hall where we could cook our own breakfast, lunch, and dinner.

The food was not bad. But the majority of people craved for rice instead of meat. We asked for rice and we got it, but they cut down the meat.

Concentration camp life was very much like the relocation camps for Japanese-Americans evacuated from the Pacific Coast. The only difference is that the camp I was in was not for Americans. No American citizens were in the camp, only Japanese subjects. We were not prisoners of war. But prisoners of war rules and regulations were applied for daily living. The camp was run in accordance with the Geneva Convention Regulations for detainees.

There was a daily routine. We woke up in the morning at six o'clock. We had breakfast between six-thirty and seven. Before lunch we were supposed to clean the compound, and later on we volunteered for some type of work around the camp, cleaning and other things. Later on we were given a certain section of land on which to grow our own vegetables, so we had time to spend raising vegetables which we used in our kitchen. Provisions were supplied by the Army. We had a kitchen for every section of between seventy-five and

---

[7] **confiscated**—taken by government authority.

a hundred people and regular rations were delivered every day.

We didn't know what was going to happen next, so the general feeling in the camp was anxiety and insecurity. The **morale**[8] was very high because we knew that we were well protected from anything that might have happened out there. The camp was way out in the desert and nobody came to bother us. We didn't have any reason to be afraid that anything would happen to us. But we didn't know what was going to happen tomorrow or the next day.

We were mostly men separated from their families. So the first concern was what the family was doing back home. Back in San Francisco, Los Angeles, or Hawaii, or even Alaska.

There was much breaking up of families. When a man with a family was apprehended and sent to camp like that, he couldn't carry on business and he didn't know what to do. So there was much anxiety and worrying, and every day there was writing home and asking them how they're getting along.

Some people experienced a bitter resentment when they were picked up by the FBI. They didn't know why they were being **apprehended**,[9] so they argued back and forth and had a very bitter experience. They had a very bitter feeling against the United States. As for myself, I thought of the United States as my second home and I lived according to the belief that I would spend the rest of my life here. I thought of the war just as a temporary thing. I was in a camp for Japanese aliens who were suspected of loyalty to Japan because they were officers of Japanese organizations in the Japanese communities.

But there was another type of camp in the United States at the same time. These were camps for the deten-

---

[8] **morale**—mental and emotional condition.

[9] **apprehended**—arrested.

tion of all Japanese-American people whether American citizens of Japanese ancestry, or Japanese subjects. All Japanese-American people living on the Pacific Coast were evacuated to relocation camps. That was done against their constitutional rights as American citizens.

Even now, years after the war is over, we still have certain unsolved questions in our minds about the Constitution—how was it possible to have American citizens in concentration camps? I sometimes wonder why we didn't protest this at the time. But we couldn't have done that because people were put in the camps by executive order of the President and we didn't have any way of protesting or demonstrating. All around the camp was a barbed-wire fence, and every hundred yards there was a watchtower with American soldiers with loaded guns and sometimes machine guns, so we didn't have any chance for a protest.

When the FBI or American soldiers came to pick us up, the first thought when they knocked at the door is, if I say no, they will just shoot us to death. We knew they were ordered to shoot. Once we were in the camps, I don't think we ever feared for our lives. We knew we would come out of there some day sooner or later, but we didn't know how long. Maybe two years, three years, some day we would come out. That was for sure, we knew that.

There was some propaganda that Japan would win the war, and if Japan won the war, well, we would take over the United States. The Japanese government would come over and we were going to have a big time. That was one rumor, of course. We took it as a joke. But there was such rough talk in the camp. Of course, since the war, this executive order was revoked and declared unconstitutional, so we have had some opportunity to educate the public that such unconstitutional racism hurts not only one group of people but the whole United States. We have certain elements in our society that have hatred against other groups of people because of difference in color or culture or something. When you have such a hatred, it's not healthy. Certainly it's not safe for anybody to live in such a society.

When I came to the United States I was educated in an American school and went to college, so I consider myself an American. In fact, I was naturalized in 1952, so I'm a bona fide American citizen. But long before that I would do anything for the United States, even risk my life.

When I was in the camp I volunteered to help win the war for the United States. I had reasons for that. The first reason was I didn't like the Emperor system—it was not good for the people of Japan. Another thing is I felt loyal to the country I adopted. By that time I was married and had children who were United States citizens so I tried to make them proud by volunteering to do something to win the war. And the United States government took me as a member of the Office of Strategic Services—the OSS. It was a secret service similar to the CIA, established by the executive order of President Roosevelt. I was involved in psychological warfare and was sent to Calcutta, India, for fieldwork. And that's where I was when the war ended. I'm very proud that I did something to win the war for the United States even though at the time I was a Japanese subject. After the war I went to Tokyo as a translator and interpreter for General MacArthur's headquarters.

QUESTIONS TO CONSIDER

1. How are the two accounts similar? How are they different?

2. If you were Roy Yano, would you have volunteered to help the United States war effort? Why or why not?

3. Do you think the internment of Japanese-Americans was justified? Why or why not?

The Navajo Code Talkers

BY WILLIAM E. HAFFORD

The war in the Pacific was largely a fight for the control of islands, many of them only a few acres in size. These islands were important because they could be used as stopping places for ships and refueling spots for airplanes. Airstrips on them could launch bombing raids against Japan.

The fight for the islands was intense and very difficult. Communication among different forces once they landed and secured themselves was very important. It was vital that these communications not be understandable to the Japanese. Code cracking had become such an art by this time in the war that both sides were routinely reading each others' messages. The Americans needed a new code. It came from the Navajo Indian Reservation.

The brisk wind that danced tumbleweeds through the sandy streets of Window Rock, Arizona, gave the pair of light-skinned strangers no exemption. It covered their sharply pressed uniforms with fine red dust and dulled the sheen of their polished shoes. An elderly Navajo man leaning against a storefront studied them as they walked. He had no trouble concluding that the clothes were government issue, but the wearers' presence in the tribal capital in the spring of 1942 was an **enigma**.[1] The high plateau country of the sprawling Navajo Indian Reservation, a land of shifting dunes and soaring buttes, was far removed from any military training facility. Curious.

The Navajo would make no inquiry of the strangers. He would wait patiently until time revealed the purpose of their visit. In due course, he learned that the two men were recruiters for the U.S. Marine Corps. What he probably did not learn until much later was that they had a very specific mission.

The recruiting visit was actually the outgrowth of a hunch that turned into an abiding conviction. Ever since the attack on Pearl Harbor the previous December, Philip Johnston, a California engineer, had been following the disturbing news from the Pacific. He heard that Japanese **cryptographers**[2] were breaking American communications codes. The enemy also had radio operators who spoke English like Iowa farmers and could infiltrate U.S. voice networks to countermand orders and otherwise confuse operations.

Johnston, the son of a missionary, had lived on the Navajo reservation as a boy, and he spoke the language. He was sure that no Japanese had ever spent enough time on the reservation to learn even a few words. Convinced that Navajo would present the enemy with an **indecipherable**[3] enigma, Philip Johnston told his idea to the Marines.

In the first months of the war, the U.S. military had received thousands of well-intentioned ideas from the

---

[1] **enigma**—mystery.

[2] **cryptographers**—specialists in writing and breaking codes.

[3] **indecipherable**—unsolvable.

civilian population, ranging from promising to wildly bizarre. The officer at Camp Elliott outside San Diego felt that Johnston's recommendation lay somewhere between those two extremes. Instead of relying on codes and the English language, Johnston suggested the Marines create a network of Navajos who would transmit messages in their native tongue. Maybe it was worth a try. Though skeptical, Washington's top brass extended permission for an experimental program.

For two days after arriving on the reservation, the recruiting team was avoided by everyone. Then First Sgt. (later Capt.) Frank Shinn approached Chee Dodge, chairman of the tribal council, and explained his purpose. Persuaded of its legitimacy, the chairman gave his approval, and the word went out over short-wave radio to every trading post on the reservation. The response was immediate. Shinn and Staff Sgt. Paul Andersen began interviewing the crowd of applicants that appeared the next morning, and within a few weeks they had selected the 30 recruits they had been authorized to enlist. Of these, 29 were inducted.

Candidates had to be fluent in both English and Navajo. Many applicants, although eager to serve, were not sufficiently bilingual; others were married with dependents, or had physical limitations.

Some of the Indians inducted had falsified their age and were actually only 15 or 16. Carl Gorman, on the other hand, was overage for initial enlistment. But when asked how old he was, Gorman said he was 28 and was handed an application. Some of the men confused the words "marine" and "submarine" and believed they were going into undersea service. A few, with only a vague idea of the geography involved, understood their ancestral lands were in imminent danger from Japanese invaders.

As the train carrying the new Marines to the West Coast sped through the night, some of the enlistees slept. Others **stoically**[4] studied the stars beyond the coach windows and pondered the suddenness of their passage into an alien world. Probably none had any concept of the violence and danger that lay ahead. And even more certainly, the Navajos, in their faded jeans and dusty boots, were oblivious to how important would be their unique role in baffling and outwitting one of the most sophisticated war machines in the world.

At boot camp, the Navajos stood out because of their dark skin, high cheekbones, and jet black hair. But soon less apparent attributes began to draw notice. Born to a **Spartan**[5] outdoor existence, they exhibited unusual endurance and accepted the rigors of basic training without complaint. They also proved to be outstanding marksmen and excelled at nighttime maneuvers.

But the most important task for the Navajos was **cerebral**,[6] not physical. Staff officers wanted an added precaution against the remote possibility the enemy might find someone who could understand Navajo. So they asked the new Marines to encode the Navajo language.

Cosey Stanley Brown, one of the original recruits, later described how they did it. "We decided to make a new Navajo language where we substituted and changed words around. We came out with a mixed-up language that not even other Navajos could understand." The ultimate safeguard lay in the fact that the code was committed to memory.

When the system was tested, experts from various intelligence units monitored the Navajos in field exercises. All confessed frustration. "It sounded like **gibberish**.[7] We couldn't even transcribe it, much less crack it,"

---

[4] **stoically**—with calm acceptance.

[5] **Spartan**—like the ancient Romans of Sparta, disciplined, without frills, frugal.

[6] **cerebral**—brain work, intellectual.

[7] **gibberish**—nonsense.

said an officer who had devoted his entire career to cryptography.

Then the Marines tried the code on a group of Navajo servicemen not in the program. "These are all Navajo words," said one, "but they don't make sense." Finally convinced, the Marine Corps quickly shipped two members of the original group back to the reservation. They wanted another 200 Navajo enlistees.

John Benally was assigned to the recruiting station at Gallup, New Mexico. John Manuelito joined Sergeants Shinn and Andersen in a recruiting trailer that traveled throughout the reservation.

By this time, the originator of the whole idea, Philip Johnston, had enlisted as a staff sergeant and was placed in charge of code talker training. Meanwhile the original group—minus the two assigned as recruiters—shipped out for the Pacific theater of operations, where they were introduced to combat in the jungles of Guadalcanal.

At first, some Marine field commanders seemed confused about the role of the Navajos and frequently used them as runners to carry messages through enemy lines. Their ability often amazed the other Marines. Said one sergeant, "They could crawl through the jungle without a sound and hide where there wasn't anywhere to hide. We always figured they knew that kind of stuff instinctively."

But courier duty came to an abrupt halt after a Marine colonel paired a team of code talkers against a pair of communications specialists who would use a typical mechanical coding cylinder.[8] The competition would determine which man on the receiving end could decode a message first. After the Navajo scrawled his message on a pad, the officer asked him how long it would take to decode. "It was decoded when I wrote it down," the Indian replied. Then, within a few minutes,

---

[8] coding cylinder—the machine used to break codes.

the code talker sent messages to four different units and received confirmation, while the man working with the standard system was still decoding the original message.

After that episode, and for the rest of the Pacific campaign, the Navajos were employed almost exclusively as code talkers. But their duty was no less dangerous than that of runners. One of the code talkers has described an experience typical of the conditions they encountered. "My buddy and I had been in this trench for four days. We had tied ourselves together with a short piece of cord so we couldn't lose each other in the dark. One night when the firing was intense, a screaming Japanese soldier leaped into the trench and killed my partner with a samurai sword before other Marines could shoot him. I had to stay there sending messages with my friend's blood gushing over me. After we got out, I was told all my messages got through without error."

Harold Foster received Purple Hearts for wounds sustained on Tarawa and Iwo Jima. Martin Napa was wounded in both legs by a Japanese machine gun on Iwo Jima, and walked with great pain for the rest of his life.

Once the code talkers' true value was recognized, their contributions escalated to handling a major portion of critical battlefield communications as American forces island-hopped across the Pacific. They performed admirably on New Britain, Bougainville, Tarawa, Guam, Iwo Jima, Okinawa, and other battlefields whose names evoke bloody memories. Col. Marlow Williams, who served as a combat commander at Bougainville, Guam, and Iwo Jima, considered the code talkers invaluable in those campaigns.

There is no way to estimate the number of American lives saved by the speed and accuracy of the Navajo code system. On Saipan, for example, Marine forces had overtaken Japanese positions so quickly that American artillery units were unaware of the swing in battle.

Suddenly, shells from U.S. guns began to fall on the newly occupied positions.

The commander radioed back, ordering the artillery to cease fire. But the batteries ignored the command, believing the message came from an English-speaking Japanese radio operator. Above the din of exploding rounds, the frontline commander frantically shouted, "Arizona," a battlefield synonym for code talker. In moments a dark-skinned figure zigzagged through the erupting terrain, jumped into the officer's foxhole, and got on the radio. The shelling stopped abruptly; although they hadn't trusted the transmission in English, the artillery officers were convinced by the **inimitable**[9] muttering of the code talker.

No code talker was ever captured by the Japanese forces. But because of their somewhat Oriental-appearing features, the Navajos were often mistaken for the enemy and challenged by their own troops. Explained one former Marine officer, "Japanese soldiers sometimes took uniforms off our dead, put them on, and tried to infiltrate our lines. I learned to introduce new men to the Navajos right away so they wouldn't mistake them. Once, near dusk, a code talker was returning from laying telephone wires, and a new man nearly shot him."

William McCabe tells of being captured by fellow Americans on Guadalcanal. "I was looking for some orange juice in a chow dump when someone put a gun in my back. He took me to the provost marshal and said, 'I've caught me a Jap that speaks pretty good English.' They didn't have any place to keep prisoners, so they started talking about shooting me. I finally convinced them to take me down to my outfit where they identified me. After that, our commanding officer assigned a white guy to be my bodyguard. He went everywhere I went." In time, it became common practice to assign bodyguards to code talkers in combat zones.

---

[9] **inimitable**—incapable of being imitated.

Throughout the Pacific campaign, the code talkers earned the accolades of high-ranking Marine officers. But Iwo Jima was surely their finest performance. The entire invasion was directed by orders communicated in Navajo code. During the first 48 hours, while the American forces were landing and consolidating shore positions, six code-talker networks operated around the clock, sending and receiving more than 800 critical messages without error. Not one word was decoded by the Japanese. Said Maj. Howard M. Conner, communications officer for the Fifth Marine Division, "Without the Navajos, the Marines would never have taken Iwo Jima."

At the **cessation**[10] of hostilities, the Marine Corps and Navy Department, believing that the Navajo code might be needed in future conflicts, kept the project classified "top secret." For 23 years, the general public knew virtually nothing of the wartime contributions made by the Navajo code talkers.

Finally, in 1968, the secret classification was dropped, and in June, 1969, the code talkers were presented specially struck medallions at a Fourth Marine Division Association reunion in Chicago.

Upon returning to the Navajo reservation at war's end, most code talkers participated in an "Enemy Way" ceremony, a ritual designed to **exorcise**[11] painful memories of battle and purify the participant.

If there is a complete roster of Navajo code talkers of World War II, it is not readily available. Most accounts indicate about 400 Navajos were involved. Seven, Harold Foster recalls, died in combat. About 230 are still living, most of them on the Navajo reservation. Peter MacDonald, who enlisted in 1944 at 15, is now chairman of the Navajo Tribal Council.[12] Carl Gorman, the oldest volunteer, later entered college, became an art instructor,

---

[10] **cessation**—ending.

[11] **exorcise**—expel evil.

[12] This article was written in 1989.

and is the father of artist R. C. Gorman. Now retired, the senior Gorman maintains a small studio near Window Rock. Eugene Roanhorse Crawford, who believes he was the first to enlist, now lives in Gallup.

Many years after the war, the former chief of intelligence for the Japanese forces remarked that his countrymen had deciphered many American codes but never that used by the Marines. When he was told that messages were transmitted in the language of an American Indian tribe, Gen. Seizo Arisue sighed and replied, "Thank you. That is a puzzle I thought would never be solved."

Many believe the Navajo code, created largely by schoolboys from a remote Indian reservation, may have been the only truly unbreakable code in the history of warfare.

QUESTIONS TO CONSIDER

1. What persuaded the marine commanders to use the Navajo marines as the code talkers they had been trained to be?

2. Why do you think their role was not immediately accepted?

3. Because the code and their activities were classified top-secret, the marines could not tell their families and friends on the reservation about their role in the war. How do you think they felt about this?

Pacific War Diary

BY JAMES FAHEY

James Fahey served as Seaman, First Class, in the Pacific, near the Solomon Islands. In spite of the military rules against diary keeping, he wrote in his regularly. Like those of other servicemen, his diary entries speak frankly about his feelings for his enemy.

Wednesday, June 30, 1943—We are still at sea. I got up at 3:15 A.M. this morning for the 4 to 8 watch. About 5:15 this morning we could see land, it was the Solomons. The rest of the ships had left us. We made our way to Tulagi[1] with the rest of Task Force 39. It is a very hot day.

. . . Late this afternoon everything was in readiness and at 6:30 P.M. Tulagi was behind us as we made our way up the Solomons. We are all by ourselves now, good old Task Force 39, Cruiser Division 12. They should call us Merrill's Lone Wolves because we operate as a small task force, without carriers, battleships or even

---

[1] Tulagi—an island in the group of South Pacific islands known as the Solomons.

heavy cruisers. We are always snooping in the Japs' back yard. We could not afford to send carriers or battleships up the Solomons because they would be easy targets for the land-based planes, and also subs that would be hiding near the jungle. We don't mind losing light cruisers and destroyers but the larger ships would not be worth the gamble, when we can do the job anyway. The Solomons are over five hundred miles long and most of the islands are Jap-held fortresses. We call this going up the slot. It is like going up an alley at night in the tough sections of any big city. You have to be on your guard at all times. You never know when a Jap sub will be up ahead of you dead in the water, just waiting to spring the trap. It is also a good hiding place for PT boats[2] and warships. The Japs also have many airfields on these islands.

We did not eat supper in the mess hall[3] tonight because we could not take the chance. We had 1 ham sandwich, 1 cookie, and 1 apple for supper at our battle stations. One of our pilots went to his battle station with a machine gun, he was very close to our mount, which is one of the highest places on the ship. If Jap planes attacked us, he wanted to get a shot at them. Capt. Tobin spoke to the crew at 7 P.M. and said we would bombard the Shortlands at 1:58 tomorrow morning.

The Japs have barracks there, a radar station, big fuel dumps, and plenty of troops plus ammunition dumps. We expect to run into big 6 inch shore guns.

Our bombardment will take place in darkness as usual right in the Japs' backyard.

It will be a bad place to get hit because if you land in the water the sharks will get you, and if you land on one of the islands the Japs will get you, and of course that means torture and death.

---

[2] PT boats—fast, light boats used to torpedo enemy ships.

[3] mess hall—dining hall.

July 1, 1943—The hours passed and we finally reached our destination. About 30 minutes before zero hour it began to rain but it did not bother us because we were going to have a ringside view of the whole show. They were not going to fire the machine guns so that would enable us to see what happened. We would have the night off, if we were needed we would begin to fire at once. The 5 and 6 inch guns will do the firing. When the word was passed for our ships to start firing on the Jap-held island we were soaking wet, and during most of the time we were here it rained. The Japs did not know what hit them as our ships sneaked in on them while they were sound asleep and ripped the place with 5 and 6 inch shells. Many a Jap died in his bunk. You could see big explosions as the ammunition dump went up. The visibility was very bad because of the rain and darkness. Our task force really poured it on the Japs as they knocked out the Jap targets and slaughtered the troops. Our battle station is only a few feet from the big guns and when they fired, the big flashes were blinding. We were so close to the guns that we could almost look down the barrels. The concussion was awful, it felt like our eardrums would be blown to bits, and the pain in our throat and chest was almost unbearable. The cotton and rubber plugs in our ears did not help, because we were too close to the guns. When these guns fire like this, they even snap the steel plates and ladders that go up to the mount. Jap shore guns opened up on us but no damage was done to our ships. While all this was going on, our ship was hit by a torpedo but lucky for us it must have been a dud. We did not know if it came from a sub or PT boat. This would have been a great place to get stranded. When we completed the bombardment Admiral Merrill ordered the task force back to its base, many hundreds of miles south of here. It rained until the sun came up on this cloudy Thursday morning of July 1, 1943. We had some peanut brittle candy for breakfast and for dinner we had two hard-boiled eggs, 1 orange, and 2 donuts. It was a cloudy day as we raced south. We were in the midst of Jap-held airfields and we never knew when they would attack us. We had three air raid warnings but the planes did not attack us. The cloudy weather must be interfering with their search for us. Everyone could stand some sleep but we will not get that, for some time. They say we might be back in a day or so for more bombardments against the Japs.

It is late in the afternoon as we pass good old Guadalcanal. The sun is out now and we were lucky it did not come out this morning, we would have made good targets for the Jap planes. My glasses broke again, but I patched them up. It is the glass that is broken.

The sun and glare from the water does a job on your eyes, it is almost blinding and lack of sleep does not help.

July 11, 1943—We are now at Purvis Bay in the Solomons, it is not too far from Tulagi. We will bombard the Japs at 3 A.M. tomorrow morning. After our bombardment our troops are to advance from 3 sides and destroy the Jap troops not killed with our bombardment and in 24 hours Munda and its important airfield will be ours.

This bombardment will also take place in the dark. Every time we go up the Slot to take on the Japs it is dark, it is near midnight or early in the morning. We get very little sleep with this schedule but it is the only way we can do it. We are not strong enough yet to do this in the daytime. We would run out of warships and our air power is not strong enough either, there are too many Jap airfields in the Solomons. We only get about 10 per cent of the war supplies down here while the European theatre of war gets about 90 per cent. We are hanging on with a big prayer.

I think the rugged routine that we have had for the past 7 months has something to do with the way the men have been acting lately. The men have noticed it themselves doing it. Your mind goes blank and you find yourself walking around some part of the ship, some distance from where you want to go, and then it dawns on you that you are not supposed to be there. You forget what day it is, what you had for breakfast, what you did in the morning. You find yourself in the washroom with no soap or towel. When you turn the water on, then it dawns on you. You forget to take your toothbrush and paste with you, until you begin to brush your teeth. You go in to take a shower without towel or soap. Some of the fellows have a lighted cigarette in their mouths and ask for a match to light theirs. When you wake up, you think it is time to go on watch, etc.

These things sneak up on you before you know it. You will find yourself somewhere and ask yourself, "What am I doing here?" Our routine for almost 7 months has not helped the situation. We spend most of our time on the ship, which is 607 ft. long and about 50 ft. at its widest point. Our recreation consists of a few hours a month in the jungle. Some of the men have not left the ship in months because there is nothing to amount to on the recreation parties. We seldom get a night's sleep. The only thing we see is, glaring ocean, thick green jungle and tropical rain storms. The heat and the tropical storms and humidity are wicked and of course the Japs always keep the pressure on us, you never know what the outcome will be when you take on the Japs. . . .

Monday, July 12, 1943— After many hours at our battle stations our task force finally reached Munda and at 3 A.M. this morning we started our bombardment on the Japs. They must have been sound asleep this early hour of the morning but it didn't take long to wake them up, the others died in their sleep. It did not take long after we opened up on the Japs, we could see great explosions. They looked like fuel and ammunition dumps, they went sky high. It was a pretty clear morning, not as dark as some of our other attacks. . . .

Thursday, November 4, 1943—I did not get any sleep until 2 A.M. this morning. We were receiving fuel from one of the tankers. They told us to get some sleep while the ship was fueling. We fell asleep on the steel deck. They woke us up in one hour at 3 A.M. when we were refueled. I did not get to bed again until 4:15 A.M. We usually crawl under a near mount or turret and fall asleep. Reveille[4] was 6 A.M. There was no resting for the weary today. All hands worked all day under a hot blazing sun, carrying tons of **ammunition**.[5] The sun gave us quite a burn because we wore no shirts to beat the head-sapping sun. We continued into the night. Even some of the officers helped. It makes you forget the heavy work that you are doing when you see the officers pitch in and help. They did not have to do this. They could be catching up with the many hours of sleep they lost. It's no joke carrying a 135 pound armor-piercing shell almost the length of a ship that is 607 ft. long. Two men are used to pick the shell up and put it on another man's shoulder which is bare. It's then carried or staggered on its way, always with the hope that it doesn't drop. Thousands of shells were carried plus the powder cases. Some of the smaller fellows could not carry the armor-piercing shells because of the extreme weight. Usually a piece of cloth on the shoulder was used in vain for the heavy shell still cuts into the bone.

A very special guest came aboard this morning. It was the brass himself, the number 1 man, Admiral "Bull"

---

[4] Reveille—the morning signal to get out of bed.

[5] **ammunition**—explosive material, bullets, shot.

Halsey. The men would do anything for him. He rates with the greatest of all time. A PT boat pulled alongside and he came aboard. He had a long handshake with Admiral Merrill on the starboard quarterdeck. Everyone wanted to get a look at the "Bull." Halsey is a tough-looking man and looks as if he could take care of one of his namesakes. He had on a pair of shorts, tan in color and a short sleeve shirt of the same color, the shirt open at the collar. You would never believe that he was the number 1 man in the South Pacific. He wants his men to be comfortable. He doesn't go in for this regulation stuff. As they were putting a six inch 135 pound armor-piercing shell on my shoulder, who was standing in front of me but "Bull" Halsey and Admiral Merrill. As he stood there watching us carry ammunition, I tried to look right through him. I tried to study him and see what he was made of. I left him standing there, with the shell on my shoulder and the knowledge that he came from good stock. It did not take long to draw that con-clusion because he had it written all over him. We got the best man in command down here in the "Bull." Admiral Merrill showed him the damage we received from the Jap bombs. Before he left the ship, he congrat-ulated everyone for the great job they did.

Francis McCarthey, the news reporter for United Press, was also aboard our ship during all this action. He was the only correspondent with the task force. When we reached Purvis Bay, he had to share his scoop with the other reporters. Mr. McCarthey should get some kind of award. It's tough when you get a scoop like this and then have to share it with several other syndicated reporters. Everyone thinks the world of Mr. McCarthey.

Thursday, November 25, 1943—Nickelson had a heat stroke from sleeping in the compartment last night. We carried him to sick bay as he was too weak and dizzy to go it alone. The flashproof cover where he lay was covered with his sweat. He was kept in sick bay for a day. I can't understand how some of the fellows sleep in the compartment, especially ours, as it's above the waterline. The sun beats against the steel sides and the deck all day. The side of the ship is so hot that you cannot touch it. On top of that, there is very little air to breathe. Sleeping there is out of the question. . . .

I was talking to one of the crewmen today. It seems that the duty here is getting the best of him. He told me that he was going crazy. He appeared very nervous. We've been in continuous action for almost a year now. Some of the younger men in the 17-year-old group wish that they were back in the States and out of the Navy. One of them is here on watch with me now. He really does look homesick. He's sorry now that he was in such a hurry to enter the service. He's only 17 years old. I told him that after a few months he would recover and the Navy would seem like a second home to him and he'd never care if he saw home again. I also told him to forget about being homesick and think of something else. I never felt lonesome in all the time we have been here, in fact I never give it a thought.

Some of the new men cannot wait to get into action. They say "I came down here to fight a war and that's what I want." It takes all kinds. After being in so many campaigns, you're disappointed if one passes you by. There's always the next one. When you find yourself in it, there's always the realization of how crazy you were in thinking that way. When this one's completed, never again. When it's finally terminated, you're always ready for the next one. It gets to be a disease after a time.

QUESTIONS TO CONSIDER

1. How does Fahey feel about the officers and high military command?

2. What effect does he say the routine has on the sailors on board ship?

3. What seems to be his philosophy of coping in the service?

"I Believe in This War"

BY J. SAUNDERS REDDING

At the time of the Second World War, American society was a segregated society. Racism was institutionalized in laws and customs that kept African Americans apart from white citizens. What the war meant to African Americans is poignantly and forcefully told here. Its legacy and its connections with the Civil War are detailed. Redding also discusses patriotism and what it meant to him.

War had no heroic traditions for me. Wars were white folks'. All wars in historical memory. The last war, and the Spanish-American War before that, and the Civil War. I had been brought up in a way that admitted of no heroics. I think my parents were right. Life for them was a fierce, bitter, soul-searching war of spiritual and economic **attrition**;[1] they fought it without heroics, but with stubborn heroism. Their heroism was screwed up to a pitch of idealism so intense that it found a safety

---

[1] **attrition**—wearing down.

valve in cynicism about the heroics of white folks' war. This cynicism went back at least as far as my **paternal**[2] grandmother, whose fierce eyes used to lash the faces of her five grandchildren as she said, "An' he done som'pin big an' brave away down dere to Chickymorgy[3] an' dey made a iron image of him 'cause he got his head blowed off an' his stomick blowed out fightin' to keep his slaves." I cannot convey the scorn and the cynicism she put into her picture of that hero-son of her slave-master, but I have never forgotten.

I was nearly ten when we entered the last war in 1917. The European fighting, and the sinking of the *Lusitania*, had seemed as remote, as distantly meaningless to us, as the Battle of Hastings.[4] Then we went in and suddenly the city was flag-draped, slogan-plastered, and as riotously gay as on circus half-holidays. I remember one fine Sunday we came upon an immense new billboard with a new slogan: GIVE! TO MAKE THE WORLD SAFE FOR DEMOCRACY. My brother, who was the oldest of us, asked what making the world safe for democracy meant. My father frowned, but before he could answer, my mother broke in.

"It's just something to say, like . . . "—and then she was stuck until she hit upon one of the family's old jokes—"like 'Let's make a million dollars.'" We all laughed, but the bitter core of her meaning lay revealed, even for the youngest of us, like the stone in a halved peach. . . .

And so, since I have reached maturity and thought a man's thoughts and had a man's—a Negro man's—experiences, I have thought that I could never believe in war again. Yet I believe in this one.

---

[2] **paternal**—on the father's side.

[3] Chickymorgy—the Civil War battle of Chickamauga.

[4] The Battle of Hastings took place in 1066. This date is the traditional beginning of modern England.

There are many things about this war that I do not like, just as there are many things about "practical" Christianity that I do not like. But I believe in Christianity, and if I accept the shoddy and unfulfilling in the conduct of this war, I do it as voluntarily and as purposefully as I accept the trash in the workings of "practical" Christianity. I do not like the odor of political pandering that arises from some groups. I do not like these "race incidents" in the camps. I do not like the world's not knowing officially that there were Negro soldiers on Bataan with General Wainwright. I do not like the constant references to the Japs as "yellow bastards," "yellow bellies," and "yellow monkeys,"[5] as if color had something to do with treachery, as if color were the issue and the thing we are fighting rather than oppression, slavery, and a way of life hateful and nauseating. These and other things I do not like, yet I believe in the war. . . .

This is a war to keep men free. The struggle to broaden and lengthen the road of freedom—our own private and important war to enlarge freedom here in America—will come later. That this private, intra-American war will be carried on and won is the only real reason we Negroes have to fight. We must keep the road open. Did we not believe in a victory in that intra-American war, we could not believe in nor stomach the compulsion of this. If we could not believe in the realization of democratic freedom for ourselves, certainly no one could ask us to die for the preservation of that ideal for others. But to broaden and lengthen the road of freedom is different from preserving it. And our first duty is to keep the road of freedom open. It must be done continuously. It is the duty of the whole people to do this. Our next duty (and this, too, is the whole people's) is to broaden the road so that more people can

[5] "yellow bastards," "yellow bellies," and "yellow monkeys"—derogatory terms used to describe the Japanese during the war.

travel it without snarling traffic. To die in these duties is to die for something. . . .

I believe in this war, finally, because I believe in the ultimate **vindication**[6] of the wisdom of the brotherhood of man. This is not foggy idealism. I think that the growing manifestations of the interdependence of all men is an argument for the wisdom of brotherhood. I think that the shrunk compass of the world is an argument. I think that the talk of united nations and of planned interdependence is an argument.

More immediately, I believe in this war because I believe in America. I believe in what America professes to stand for. Nor is this, I think, whistling in the dark. There are a great many things wrong here. There are only a few men of good will. I do not lose sight of that. I know the inequalities, the outraged hopes and faith, the inbred hate; and I know that there are people who wish merely to lay these by in the closet of the national mind until the crisis is over. But it would be equally foolish for me to lose sight of the advances that are made, the barriers that are leveled, the privileges that grow. Foolish, too, to remain blind to the distinction that exists between simple race prejudice, already growing **moribund**[7] under the impact of this war, and theories of racial superiority as a basic **tenet**[8] of a societal system—theories that at bottom are the avowed justification for suppression, defilement and murder.

I will take this that I have here. I will take the democratic theory. The bit of road of freedom that stretches through America is worth fighting to preserve. The very fact that I, a Negro in America, can fight against the evils in America is worth fighting for. This open fighting against the wrongs one hates is the mark and the hope of democratic freedom. I do not underestimate the

---

[6] **vindication**—proof.

[7] **moribund**—in a dying state.

[8] **tenet**—belief.

struggle. I know the learning that must take place, the evils that must be broken, the depths that must be climbed. But I am free to help in doing these things. I count. I am free (though only a little as yet) to pound blows at the huge body of my American world until, like a **chastened**[9] mother, she gives me nurture with the rest.

---

[9] **chastened**—having learned one's lesson; humbled.

QUESTIONS TO CONSIDER

1. Why do you think war has no heroic traditions for Redding? What war heroes did he hear about growing up?

2. What does Redding not like about this war?

3. What does he mean when he says the interdependence of all men is an argument for the wisdom of the brotherhood of man?

4. What does he mean when he says there is a difference between "simple race prejudice" and "theories of racial superiority as a basic tenet of a societal system"? What societal system is he referring to?

5. Why do you think Redding believes in this war?

War in the Pacific

▲
Air Strike The attack on Pear Harbor sunk or damaged 18 ships and about 190 planes. Other casualties were the more than 2,400 who died and 1,178 who were wounded in the attack. Here Japanese Mitsubishi divebombers are warming up on the deck of an aircraft carrier shortly before the attack.

Waiting for Battle Soldiers reported in their wartime diaries the endless waiting in war. To pass the time, soldiers often read magazines, played cards, or wrote home to friends or loved ones.

▲

Waiting for a Ride Transporting soldiers was in itself a major effort. Soldiers often spent long stretches moving from one station or camp to another, and often they took any ride available.

▲

Ready for Battle Soldiers moved into battle-ready positions and often waited for hours until the signal was given to attack.

Heat of the Battle Pictures convey better than words the feeling of being in a battle. Here, in Saipan, a marine is running to avoid being hit by shrapnel from incoming enemy fire. ▶

▲

Navajo Code Talkers Here American Indian Marines in a jungle in the Pacific send a message in Navajo to avoid the interception and deciphering of the message by the Japanese.

▲

Navy Throughout the war, the U.S. Navy worked in concert with other branches of the military. Naval battles like this one were critical to the U.S. victory in the Pacific.

War Ends

The Last Days of Hitler

BY HUGH TREVOR-ROPER

For years following the war there was controversy surrounding Hitler's end. Historian Hugh Trevor-Roper takes pains in his account to establish that there were several witnesses to the events he records.

When von Below left the Bunker, Hitler was already preparing for the end. During the day the last news from the outside world had been brought in. Mussolini was dead. Hitler's partner in crime, the herald of Fascism, who had first shown to Hitler the possibilities of dictatorship in modern Europe, and had preceded him in the stages of disillusion and defeat, had now illustrated in a signal manner the fate which fallen tyrants must expect. Captured by partisans during the general uprising of northern Italy, Mussolini and his mistress Clara Petacci had been executed, and their bodies suspended by the feet in the market-place of Milan to be beaten and pelted by the **vindictive**[1] crowd. If the full details were ever known to them, Hitler and Eva Braun[2] could only have repeated the orders they had already given: their bodies were to be destroyed "so that nothing remains"; "I will not fall into the hands of an enemy who requires a new spectacle to divert his hysterical masses." In fact it is improbable that these details were reported, or could have strengthened an already firm decision. The fate of defeated **despots**[3] has generally been the same; and Hitler, who had himself exhibited the body of a field-marshal on a meat-hook, had no need of remote historical examples or of a new and dramatic instance, to know the probable fate of his own corpse, if it should be found.

In the afternoon, Hitler had his favourite Alsatian dog, Blondi, destroyed. Professor Haase, his former surgeon, who was now tending the wounded in his clinic in Berlin, had come round to the Bunker and killed it with poison. The two other dogs belonging to the household were shot by the sergeant who looked after them. After this, Hitler gave poison-capsules to his two secretaries for use in extremity.[4] He was sorry, he had said, to give them no better parting gift; and praising them for their courage he had added, characteristically, that he wished his generals were as reliable as they.

In the evening, while the inhabitants of the two outer bunkers were dining in the general dining-passage of the Fuehrerbunker,[5] they were visited by one of the S.S. guard, who informed them that the Fuehrer wished to say good-bye to the ladies and that no one was to go to bed till orders had been received. At about half-past two

---

[1] **vindictive**—looking for revenge.

[2] Eva Braun—a German actress who was first Hitler's mistress, then his wife.

[3] **despots**—tyrants.

[4] in extremity—when the absolute end comes.

[5] Fuehrerbunker—Hitler's fortified hiding place.

in the morning the orders came. They were summoned by telephone to the Bunker, and gathered again in the same general dining-passage, officers and women, about twenty persons in all. When they were assembled, Hitler came in from the private part of the Bunker, accompanied by Bormann.[6] His look was abstracted, his eyes glazed over with that film of moisture which Hanna Reitsch had noticed. Some of those who saw him even suggested that he had been drugged; but no such explanation is needed of a condition upon which more familiar observers had often commented. He walked in silence down the passage and shook hands with all the women in turn. Some spoke to him, but he said nothing, or mumbled inaudibly. Ceremonies of silent hand-shaking had become quite customary in the course of that day.

When he had left, the participants in this strange scene remained for a while to discuss its significance. They agreed that it could have one meaning only. The suicide of the Fuehrer was about to take place. Thereupon an unexpected thing happened. A great and heavy cloud seemed to roll away from the spirits of the Bunker-dwellers. The terrible sorcerer, the tyrant who had charged their days with intolerable melodramatic tension, would soon be gone, and for a brief twilight moment they could play. In the canteen of the Chancellery, where the soldiers and orderlies took their meals, there was a dance. The news was brought; but no one allowed that to interfere with the business of pleasure. A message from the Fuehrerbunker told them to be quieter; but the dance went on. A tailor who had been employed in the Fuehrer's headquarters, and who was now immured with the rest in the Chancellery, was surprised when Brigadefuehrer Rattenhuber, the head of the police guard and a general in the S.S., slapped

---

[6] Martin Bormann was a Nazi official who served as Hitler's private secretary.

him cordially on the back and greeted him with democratic familiarity. In the strict hierarchy of the Bunker the tailor felt bewildered. It was as if he had been a high officer. "It was the first time I had ever heard a high officer say 'good evening'," he said; "so I noticed that the mood had completely changed." Then, from one of his equals, he learned the reason of this sudden and irregular **affability**.[7] Hitler had said goodbye, and was going to commit suicide. There are few forces so **solvent**[8] of class distinctions as common danger, and common relief.

Though Hitler might already be preparing for death, there was still one man at least in the Bunker who was thinking of life: Martin Bormann. If Bormann could not persuade the German armies to come and rescue Hitler and himself, at least he would insist on revenge. Shortly after the farewell ceremony, at a quarter-past three in the morning of 30th April, he sent another of those telegrams in which the neurosis of the Bunker is so vividly preserved. It was addressed to Doenitz[9] at Ploen; but Bormann no longer trusted the ordinary communications, and sent it through the Gauleiter of Mecklenburg. It ran:

DOENITZ!—Our impression grows daily stronger that the divisions in the Berlin theatre have been standing idle for several days. All the reports we receive are controlled, suppressed, or distorted by Keitel. In general we can only communicate through Keitel. The Fuehrer orders you to proceed at once, and mercilessly, against all traitors.—BORMANN.

A postscript contained the words: "The Fuehrer is alive, and is conducting the defence of Berlin." These words, containing no hint of the approaching end—indeed seeming to deny its imminence—suggest that Bormann was reluctant even now to admit that his

---

[7] **affability**—friendliness.

[8] **solvent**—removing, dissolving.

[9] Admiral Karl Doenitz was Hitler's designated successor.

power would soon be over, or must be renewed from another, less calculable source.

Later in the same morning, when the new day's work had begun, the generals came as usual to the Bunker with their military reports. Brigadefuehrer Mohnke, the commandant of the Chancellery, announced a slight improvement: the Schlesischer railway station had been recaptured from the Russians; but in other aspects the military situation was unchanged. By noon the news was worse again. The underground railway tunnel in the Friedrichstrasse was reported in Russian hands; the tunnel in the Vosstrasse, close to the Chancellery, was partly occupied; the whole area of the Tiergarten had been taken; and Russian forces had reached the Potsdamer Platz and the Weidendammer Bridge over the river Spree. Hitler received these reports without emotion. At about two o'clock he took lunch. Eva Braun was not there; evidently she did not feel hungry, or ate alone in her room; and Hitler shared his meal, as usually in her absence, with his two secretaries and the cook. The conversation indicated nothing unusual. Hitler remained quiet, and did not speak of his intentions. Nevertheless, preparations were already being made for the approaching ceremony.

In the morning, the guards had been ordered to collect all their rations for the day, since they would not be allowed to pass through the corridor of the Bunker again; and about lunch-time Hitler's S.S. adjutant Sturmbannfuehrer Guensche, sent an order to the transport officer and chauffeur, Sturmbannfuehrer Erich Kempka, to send 200 litres of petrol[10] to the Chancellery garden. Kempka protested that it would be difficult to find so large a quantity at once, but he was told that it must be found. Ultimately he found about 180 litres and sent it round to the garden. Four men carried it in

---

[10] 200 litres of petrol equals approximately 52.8 gallons of gasoline.

jerricans[11] and placed it at the emergency exit of the Bunker. There they met one of the police guards, who demanded an explanation. They told him that it was for the ventilating plant. The guard told them not to be silly, for the plant was oil-driven. At this moment Hitler's personal servant, Heinz Linge, appeared. He reassured the guard, terminated the argument, and dismissed the men. Soon afterwards all the guards except those on duty were ordered to leave the Chancellery, and to stay away. It was not intended that any casual observer should witness the final scene.

Meanwhile Hitler had finished lunch, and his guests had been dismissed. For a time he remained behind; then he emerged from his suite, accompanied by Eva Braun, and another farewell ceremony took place. Bormann and Goebbels were there, with Burgdorf, Krebs, Hewel, Naumann, Voss, Rattenhuber, Hoegl, Guensche, Linge, and the four women, Frau Christian, Frau Junge, Fraeulein Krueger, and Fraeulein Manzialy.[12] Frau Goebbels was not present. Unnerved by the approaching death of her children, she remained all day in her own room. Hitler and Eva Braun shook hands with them all, and then returned to their suite. The others were dismissed, all but the high-priests and those few others whose services would be necessary. These waited in the passage. A single shot was heard. After an interval they entered the suite. Hitler was lying on the sofa, which was soaked with blood. He had shot himself through the mouth. Eva Braun was also on the sofa, also dead. A revolver was by her side, but she had not used it; she had swallowed poison. The time was half-past three.

Shortly afterwards, Artur Axmann, head of the Hitler Youth, arrived at the Bunker. He was too late for

---

[11] jerricans—flat-sided containers used for storing and carrying liquid. They hold about 19 liters (5 gallons) each.

[12] Bormann and Goebbels...Fraeulein Manzialy—This group includes Hitler's closest advisors, friends, and secretaries.

the farewell ceremony, but he was admitted to the private suite to see the dead bodies. He examined them, and stayed in the room for some minutes, talking with Goebbels. Then Goebbels left, and Axmann remained for a short while alone with the dead bodies. Outside, in the Bunker, another ceremony was being prepared: the Viking funeral.

After sending the petrol to the garden, Kempka had walked across to the Bunker by the subterranean passage which connected his office in the Hermann Goeringstrasse with the Chancellery buildings. He was greeted by Guensche with the words, "The Chief is dead." At that moment the door of Hitler's suite was opened, and Kempka too became a participant in the funeral scene.

While Axmann was meditating among the corpses, two S.S. men, one of them Hitler's servant Linge, entered the room. They wrapped Hitler's body in a blanket, concealing the bloodstained and shattered head, and carried it out into the passage, where the other observers easily recognised it by the familiar black trousers. Then two other S.S. officers carried the body up the four flights of stairs to the emergency exit, and so out into the garden. After this, Bormann entered the room, and took up the body of Eva Braun. Her death had been tidier, and no blanket was needed to conceal the evidence of it. Bormann carried the body into the passage, and then handed it to Kempka, who took it to the foot of the stairs. There it was taken from him by Guensche; and Guensche in turn gave it to a third S.S. officer, who carried it too upstairs to the garden. As an additional precaution, the other door of the Bunker, which led into the Chancellery, and some of the doors leading from the Chancellery to the garden, had been hastily locked against possible intruders.

Unfortunately, the most careful precautions are sometimes unavailing; and it was as a direct result of this precaution that two unauthorised persons in fact witnessed the scene from which it was intended to exclude them. One of the police guards, one Erich Mansfeld, happened to be on duty in the concrete observation tower at the corner of the Bunker, and noticing through the opaque, sulphurous air a sudden, suspicious scurrying of men and shutting of doors, he felt it his duty to investigate. He climbed down from his tower into the garden and walked round to the emergency exit to see what was afoot. In the porch he collided with the emerging funeral procession. First there were two S.S. officers carrying a body wrapped in a blanket, with black-trousered legs protruding from it. Then there was another S.S. officer carrying the unmistakable corpse of Eva Braun. Behind them were the mourners—Bormann, Burgdorf, Goebbels, Guensche, Linge, and Kempka. Guensche shouted at Mansfeld to get out of the way quickly; and Mansfeld, having seen the forbidden but interesting spectacle, returned to his tower.

After this interruption, the ritual was continued. The two corpses were placed side by side, a few feet from the porch, and petrol from the cans was poured over them. A Russian bombardment[13] added to the strangeness and danger of the ceremony, and the mourners withdrew for some protection under the shelter of the porch. There Guensche dipped a rag in petrol, set it alight, and flung it out upon the corpses. They were at once enveloped in a sheet of flame. The mourners stood to attention, gave the Hitler salute, and withdrew again into the Bunker, where they dispersed. Guensche afterwards described the spectacle to those who had missed it. The burning of Hitler's body, he said, was the most terrible experience in his life.

---

[13] bombardment—bomb attack, probably an air raid.

Meanwhile yet another witness had observed the spectacle. He was another of the police guards, and he too came accidentally upon the scene in consequence of the precautions which should have excluded him. His name was Hermann Karnau. Karnau, like others of the guard who were not on duty, had been ordered away from the Bunker by an officer of the S.S. Escort, and had gone to the Chancellery canteen; but after a while, in spite of his orders, he had decided to return to the Bunker. On arrival at the door of the Bunker, he had found it locked. He had therefore made his way out into the garden, in order to enter the Bunker by the emergency exit. As he turned the corner by the tower where Mansfeld was on duty, he was surprised to see two bodies lying side by side, close to the door of the Bunker. Almost at the same instant they burst, spontaneously it seemed, into flame. Karnau could not explain this sudden **combustion.**[14] He saw no one, and yet it could not be the result of enemy fire, for he was only three feet away. "Possibly someone threw a match from the doorway," he suggested; and his suggestion is essentially correct.

Karnau watched the burning corpses for a moment. They were easily recognizable, though Hitler's head was smashed. The sight, he says, was "repulsive in the extreme." Then he went down into the Bunker by the emergency exit. In the Bunker he met Sturmbannfuehrer Franz Schedle, the officer commanding the S.S. Escort. Schedle had recently been injured in the foot by a bomb. He was distracted with grief. "The Fuehrer is dead," he said; "he is burning outside"; and Karnau helped him to limp away.

---

[14] **combustion**—sudden burning.

QUESTIONS TO CONSIDER

1. Why do you think Hitler made arrangements to have his body be destroyed?

2. How do you explain the differences in people's reactions to Hitler's death?

3. In your opinion, did Trevor-Roper provide enough evidence to make you believe the events he described really happened?

Hiroshima Survivors: Yamaguchi and Hirata

BY ROBERT TRUMBULL

After the Allied forces won the battle for Guadalcanal, Japanese advances in the Pacific were stopped. With the victory in the Phillippines and the destruction of the Japanese navy at Leyte Gulf, the next step for the Allies was a land invasion of Japan itself. The planners knew from experience that, although they would win, the cost in human lives would be enormous. Projections were upwards of half a million Allied lives alone. The atomic bomb, which scientists had been working on in the United States since the early years of the war, was tested and found to work. Truman issued a warning to the Japanese, but it was ignored. So, on August 6, 1945, the United States dropped an atomic bomb on Hiroshima. Three days later, Nagasaki was bombed. This account is based on interviews with two who survived the bombing.

It was with elation that Tsutomu Yamaguchi rose early on August 6. This was to be his last day in Hiroshima; tomorrow he would be back with his wife and child in Nagasaki. His three-month assignment at the Hiroshima yard of the Mitsubishi shipbuilding company, where he had been sent from company headquarters to design a new 5,000-ton tanker, was now completed. Today he planned to finish up his affairs at the office, and tomorrow morning be on a train for Nagasaki.

Yamaguchi lived in a boarding house owned by the company. He said good-by to the proprietor and his wife, an aged couple, put on his shoes in high spirits, and took a bus. He was getting off the bus when he realized, with annoyance, that he had forgotten his "inkan," or personal seal. A Japanese office worker can't move without his inkan; dipped in red ink paste, it has to be affixed to every document that comes beneath his hand, taking the place of a handwritten signature or initials. Frowning, Yamaguchi returned to the boarding house, took off his shoes at the entrance, and accepted the elderly proprietor's invitation to a cup of tea.

Shod again—Japanese spend more time in a day taking off and putting on shoes than a Westerner does in shaving—Yamaguchi was again on his way to the office, this time by streetcar. He noted that it was another fine day, already becoming hot. As he left the streetcar to finish his journey afoot he removed his jacket and rolled up his shirt sleeves. This he later regretted.

Yamaguchi had crossed a short bridge across a small creek and was walking along an empty road bordered by potato patches when he saw a woman coming toward him, wearing the black mompé—a shapeless dark uniform with gathered trousers—that was the universal garb of Japanese women during the **austere**[1] war years.

---

[1] **austere**—without frills.

As they came abreast, the silence was broken by the faint **drone**[2] of an airplane. Yamaguchi and the woman stopped and looked up at the blue sky.

It was a bomber, Yamaguchi saw, flying at high altitude. As he watched, a small object dropped from the belly of the plane. Above the falling speck a white dot appeared. A parachute, Yamaguchi thought.

"Suddenly there was a flash like the lighting of a huge magnesium[3] flare," Yamaguchi recalls.

The young ship designer was so well drilled in air-raid precautions technique that he reacted automatically. He flung his hands to his head, covering his eyes with his fingers and stopping his ears with his two thumbs. Simultaneously he dropped to the ground, face down. But the woman in the black mompé, reacting in panic, turned and ran into the potato field.

"As I **prostrated**[4] myself, there came a terrific explosion," Yamaguchi said later. The shattering blast was followed by a convulsion of the earth that lifted the muscular young man about two feet from the ground. He felt "a strong wind" pass between his body and the roadbed.

Yamaguchi did not know whether it was the initial shock that had hurled him into the air, or the blow as he fell back to the hard earth, that dazed him. He is sure that he felt nothing as his body struck the ground.

"How long I lay in the road, dazed, I don't know," he said. "But when I opened my eyes, it was so dark all around me that I couldn't see a thing. It was as if it had suddenly become midnight in the heat of the day. When my eyes became adjusted to the darkness, I perceived that I was enveloped in an endless cloud of dust so thick it was black."

---

[2] **drone**—low humming sound.

[3] magnesium—a metal that burns with a bright, white flame.

[4] **prostrated**—lay face down.

Then the gale, as air rushed into the vacuum created by the fireball, whipped around Yamaguchi's face and quickly dispersed the pall of dust so that he could see dimly, as in a cloudy twilight.

"As the dust blew away and my surroundings became visible, I saw what seemed to be thousands of tiny, flickering lamps all over the street and in the fields. They were little circles of flame, each about the size of a doughnut. **Myriads**[5] of them were hanging on the leaves of the potato plants.

"I couldn't see the woman anywhere."

As Yamaguchi sat up, slowly recovering from his daze and bewildered by the inexplicable scene around him, he was suddenly conscious of heat. His entire body throbbed with it.

The pain was sharp on the left side of his face and in his left arm. He discovered that the exposed skin on the left side of his face and on his bare left arm, the side toward the explosion, was severely burned.

Later, Yamaguchi calculated that his distance from the center of the blast, when he fell, was about a mile and a fifth. At half this distance, the heat emanating from the fireball had melted the granite on building surfaces. It can be **surmised**[6] that the woman in the black mompé, who was upright and therefore had exposed her entire body to the heat rays, and who in addition wore a heat-absorbent color, most probably did not survive.

"I looked toward the city and saw a huge, mushroom-shaped cloud rising high into the sky. It was an immense, evil-looking pillar. It seemed to be reflecting every shade in the spectrum, turning first one color and then another."

As Yamaguchi contemplated the strange cloud, he began to feel faint. From this and his subsequent

---

[5] **myriads**—vast numbers.
[6] **surmised**—guessed.

symptoms, it seems likely that he had suffered a heavy dose of radiation. There flashed into his still-dazed mind a picture of his wife and child, and he felt suddenly a desperate urge to go to them in Nagasaki, even if he had to walk all the way.

Yamaguchi's next feeling, he recalls, was one of intense uneasiness. "I sensed," he said, "that for some reason, which I didn't analyze, it would be gravely dangerous for me to remain where I was on the road. Feeling terribly weak, and suffering intense pain from the deep burns on my face and arm, I stumbled into the potato field. There was a big tree out in the field, and I headed for that. Sometimes I could only crawl, creeping from bush to bush.

"When I finally reached the tree, I had no more strength to go on. And I had acquired a terrible thirst."

As he rested beneath the tree, Yamaguchi examined the changed landscape. Most of the scattered houses in the vicinity had collapsed as if they had been struck a sharp blow with an immense hammer. As he gazed at the shattered remains of the buildings, flames began to spurt from the fallen timbers.

Not far from the tree stood a small factory of the kind found in great numbers throughout Japan during the war years, when virtually the entire population was engaged in producing for military needs. The door facing Yamaguchi opened, and five boys, fifteen or sixteen years old, came running out. They were unclothed except for torn underpants, and they were covered with blood. Yamaguchi saw that they were crying. He forgot his own discomfort, and motioned to the boys to come to the tree. The air had turned intensely hot.

"As the boys came near, I saw that they were pale, and shaking severely," he said. "Sobbing and terrified, they told me that the small factory had taken a 'direct bomb hit,' and that everyone else inside was dead.

"I had never seen such a horrifying sight as those five shivering boys. Blood was pouring in streams from deep cuts all over their bodies, mingling with their perspiration, and their skin was burned deep red, like the color of cooked lobsters. At first it seemed, strangely, that their burned and lacerated backs and chests were growing green grass! Then I saw that hundreds of blades of sharp grass had been driven deep into their flesh, evidently by the force of the blast."

The only thing Yamaguchi could think of to help the boys was to advise them to pull the blades of grass from each other's flesh. More than their pain, they were obsessed with thirst, as was Yamaguchi himself.

"There was a brook nearby," said Yamaguchi, "running clear water, but I thought it might somehow be dangerous to drink the water, and I tried to persuade the boys to stay away from it. But as soon as they noticed the brook they rushed toward it. I don't know what became of them afterward."

Alone again, Yamaguchi once more experienced a strong feeling of unexplainable fear that told him to leave the place where he was. Some instinct urged him that the open space was dangerous. Looking about, he espied an empty rifle range used by the Army, about 300 yards from the tree where he sat. At the end of the range was a man-made trench, about six feet deep and 200 feet long, where the targets were handled.

With an impulse to take shelter, Yamaguchi got to his feet, stumbled painfully across the smoking potato field, and lowered himself into the trench.

As he slid inside, he saw that he was not alone. A woman, naked, was lying on the ground, moaning faintly.

"As I approached her, I saw that she had severe burns all over, and that her skin was the same deep-red lobster color as the boys'. When she saw me she tried to rise, but she was too weak. She mumbled, 'Help me!' I noted that she was a Korean.

"When I bent over her to see if there was anything I could do, she said piteously, 'Am I going to die?' All I could do was assure her that she was going to be all right. But as I looked at her, baked all over as she was, I was sure that her condition was hopeless.

"'Stay in the shade of the trench,' I told her. 'Don't let the sun touch your skin.'"

Now Yamaguchi was joined in the trench by two young men in the black uniforms of students. They sat down beside him. He saw, wonderingly, that they had not been hurt.

"You've got a serious burn, sir," one of the students said to the ship designer. Touching his own face, Yamaguchi could tell that his skin was highly inflamed; it seemed as if it was about to peel off. His burned left arm was black, and swelling.

"One of the boys brought from his bag a small glass jar of medicine for burns, that he said his mother had put in the bag as he was leaving home for his work in the factory that morning. He offered the medicine to me and I refused, but he insisted on opening the jar and anointing my burned skin. It felt soothing, like palm oil. I never learned that boy's name, but I feel grateful to him to this day," Yamaguchi said, relating the story ten years later.

It was now nearly noon, and Yamaguchi thought he had better continue to his office, where he expected his fellow workers might be worried about him. On the way, he passed a number of dead bodies along the roadside.

Where once had been the building housing the design section of the Mitsubishi plant, Yamaguchi found only a pile of collapsed timbers. And these had begun to burn. The beach, where the temporary structure had stood, was dotted with dead bodies of Korean laborers. Yamaguchi learned that two of his fellow workers in the design section had been killed. The survivors crowded around and embraced him in turn, then took him to the company aid station.

"I found the aid station surrounded by dead bodies, or I should say 'charred' bodies, for I had no way of telling whether the unfortunate people were actually alive or dead. They were all black. I think some were alive, for I saw slight movements of hands and feet. The medical personnel were plastering the bodies with a white ointment, turning the skin from black to white.

"They put the white ointment on my burned arm and face, and wound bandages over it, and I returned to my office mates, who were standing around in a pine grove. There I was handed an emergency ration of two small biscuits and some water. I was very hungry, but after swallowing a bit of the biscuit I immediately vomited. After that I only drank the water.

"Meanwhile, I could see Hiroshima, two miles away, burning fiercely. Many of the office girls were crying because they could not go home."

At the accounting office, Kenshi Hirata put his biscuit ration in his cloth "emergency bag," and decided to take it to his wife. In the hours since the blast, there had been much confused discussion of the bomb. They all knew now that it was some kind of super-explosive, because it was obvious, from the absence of a crater, that nothing had fallen anywhere near the Mitsubishi plant. Yet the injuries and damage were as if a direct hit had been scored nearby. A rumor spread that some of the leaflets dropped by the Americans previously had warned of a special attack on Hiroshima August 6, but no one had actually seen one of these.

Reflecting on this, Hirata set out to walk home.

"There was not a house standing as far as I could see," he said later. "Everything had burned down, or collapsed in the blast. Although I knew the city well, it was actually difficult to find my way, for all the familiar landmarks were gone, and the streets I had often walked were now buried in debris and ashes. It was not like walking in streets at all; it was more like crossing a big burnt field."

Hirata noticed, with a little shock, that there wasn't a living being in sight. "It was as if the people who had lived in this uncanny city had been reduced to ashes with their houses," he said.

As he moved slowly through the smoking waste, he soon came upon the first ghastly dead.

"The first was a little boy," he recalls. "He was completely naked, his skin was all peeled off as if he had been flayed, and the nails were falling from the ends of his fingers. His flesh was all deep red. When I first saw him I wasn't sure that I was looking at a human being."

There was the same eerie quality about other bodies, lying twisted and still in the wreckage, "looking neither alive nor dead."

Hirata was accustomed to walking from his office to his home in about fifty minutes, but today it took him over an hour and a half to pick his way through the jumbled wreckage of the burned city. He was thinking unceasingly of his wife, Setsuko, and wondering about the fate of their house, a pretty two-storied structure surrounded by a tiled wall. He noticed that perspiration was flowing down his body "like a waterfall," yet somehow he did not feel warm.

Suddenly he stopped. At this spot, he thought he should be at his house. But there was no house there, only a smoking field of ash and embers. Dirty water gushed from a pipe broken off at the ground. Poking around in the ashes, for he was sure this was the site of his house, he found remnants of an iron stove that had heated the bath water for the deep wooden tub, and some broken pieces of tile. Then he discovered some twisted metal that looked as if it might be the remains of kitchen utensils. Now he knew that this was where his house had been.

QUESTIONS TO CONSIDER

1. Several factors probably saved Yamaguchi's life. What were they?

2. What suggested to the survivors that this was not an ordinary bomb?

3. Truman believed he was saving five to ten times as many lives as those lost in the bombing of Hiroshima and Nagasaki. Do you think he was justified in dropping the atomic bomb?

An Ambulance Driver Recalls the Bergen Belsen Concentration Camp

BY NORMAN SHETHAR

The Allied forces in Eastern Europe learned first-hand of the atrocities of the Holocaust as they rescued the survivors of the concentration camps. Norman Shethar was among the troops who freed the prisoners at Bergen Belsen concentration camp. Years later, in a 1993 speech, he describes what he found and tries to understand how people could do what was done there.

I was asked to speak to you because one of my ambulance driving assignments was to carry inmates of the Bergen Belsen concentration camp from their wretched huts, where they lay in their own filth, skeletons barely breathing, to the barracks that had housed the guards and the administrative staff of the camp. The English liberating forces turned these spacious barracks into temporary hospitals. There the inmates were washed; dusted with DDT;[1] given typhus[2] shots, and their first real food. For hundreds rescue came too late, and they died in the barracks. But many more thousands were saved.

Meanwhile, outside, for almost two weeks the former Nazi guards, with machine guns covering their every move, bulldozed huge deep pits and then bulldozed the piles of bodies, at least three or four meters high and ten meters long[3] into the pits. What I want you to remember is that those guards were also ordinary people. I have to admit that I find it hard not to think of them as beasts, and at the time I certainly did think that; now I don't think they really were. It was just that they were encouraged to let loose the worst parts of their character. It couldn't have been easy for them.

I've never seen any reference to it, but in the basement of most of the barracks, I think in the bathrooms, but I can't remember for sure, there were rectangular porcelain tubs about $1^1/4$ meters[4] high standing against the wall. They were about a meter wide and extended about $1/2$ meter from the wall. There was a wide drain hole at the bottom of each one; and there was a handgrip screwed into the wall at about chest height above each side of the tubs. I can only guess that these were **vomitoriums**.[5] And I can only guess that they showed that just about everyone involved with the administration

---

[1] DDT—chemical that kills insects.

[2] typhus—a disease transmitted by fleas, lice, or mites.

[3] three or four meters high and ten meters long—ten to thirteen feet high and thirty-three feet long.

[4] about 1 1/4 meters—a little over four feet.

[5] **vomitoriums**—places for people to throw up.

of the camp drank a lot to try to deaden his own horror of what he was doing.

Working in the camp made me want to drink a lot too. Since my fellow ambulance drivers also started drinking, I guess we were all reacting about the same way. We were seeing pain on a scale none of us had ever dreamed of.

Added to that, in trying to help, we caused a lot of extra pain. Most inmates spoke no language we could understand and understood no language we could speak. Our ambulances held only four stretchers at a time. When we went into the huts we were faced with up to 750 people lying in several inches of muck; people so thin you wondered how they could be alive. We were only 120 ambulances, and we had tens of thousands of people to move. We were in a hurry, and we didn't know how to communicate with the people we were trying to save. The only way we could operate was to move the next four people we came to. That often meant separating people from their only human connection. Maybe a relative. Maybe a person from the same town; but even if no other connection, at least a neighbor in misery. After a day or two, that didn't matter to us. Despite their cries and their obvious terror, we just loaded the next four people onto our stretchers and carried them away. I'm sure that those desperate people thought we were just new guards ready to do them some new kind of injury.

To me, these people, my patients, became objects: not people. We couldn't think of them as human beings, individuals with their own personalities and their own histories; their own rights to be considered and cared for. No. We didn't have the emotional strength or the time to offer them that basic sympathy. We tried to help—we did help—but on our own terms.

I'm not painting a very pretty picture of us, the rescuers. In some ways the differences between hurting people when you're doing a job that in the long run helps them, as we were doing, and hurting people when you're just doing your job, which in the long run kills them, as the guards were doing, is not that great.

There wasn't much difference between the **callousness**[6] we developed toward the people we were trying to help, on the one hand, and the people the Allies referred to in the Post-War years, with a sneer, as the "Good" Germans, the people who were not Nazi Party members but who closed their eyes and ears and minds to what was going on around them; who never asked about the neighbors who disappeared and who turned away from the dark, locked trains that rumbled past in the night.

We drivers, at least most of us, in the hardness we quickly developed, undoubtedly had more in common with those "good" Germans than we did with the people we were rescuing.

I think about this a lot these days. In the middle of N.Y. City, where I live, there are beggars on nearly every block. Most of them are black; many are alcoholics or drug users; many are crazy; and they're all miserable. But it doesn't take many days to get very tough minded about walking right past them and just wishing they'd go away. In Europe you don't have, or at least I don't see, so many beggars; but you do have the Bosnians[7] on your consciences. It's hard for me to understand how European governments, apparently reflecting the wishes of their voters, can go on doing nothing to stop, or at least to take some active measures to oppose, the "ethnic cleansing" going on in their own community.

Doing nothing is what the "good" Germans did. All around us there are many opportunities for us all to be

---

[6] **callousness**—lack of feeling.

[7] At the time this speech was delivered, there was regular news of Serb atrocities against Muslims in Bosnia. This activity was called "ethnic cleansing" because the Serbs were trying to remove people of a different ethnic background than theirs from a region they believed was historically theirs.

"good" Germans, and I'm sorry to say that we all take advantage of most of those opportunities.

Do you know the name Adolf Eichmann? He had the purely administrative but extremely important job in the Nazi years of managing the transportation of Jews from the towns where they were arrested to the concentration camps, and the transportation of prisoners from one camp to another. The logistics were **formidable**.[8] He had to compete with the army for locomotives and freight cars, and he had to fight competing bureaucracies and bureaucratic inefficiencies every step of the way. But he worked hard at his bureaucratic job, and be performed it very efficiently.

He escaped from Germany at the end of the War, but in 1960 Israeli undercover commandos discovered this man living in Argentina under a false name. They captured him and took him to Jerusalem to stand trial as a war criminal. The trial got intense news coverage in the U.S., and I think probably throughout the Western World. A political philosopher named Hannah Arendt, who was born in Hanover, fled from Nazi Germany in the early 1930s, and came to America in 1941, attended the trial. She wrote a book about it called, "Eichmann in Jerusalem: A Report on the Banality of Evil." It's a fascinating book that says what I've been telling you. The difference is that she said it first. She made me understand myself and my own reactions to Bergen Belsen much more clearly than I had before.

The libraries are full of wonderful books that we'd enjoy and that would do us a lot of good to read. This is one of them. It's a wise and compassionate book. I recommend it to you with the full knowledge that if even two of you read it I'll be happily surprised. And I think that the two of you who read it will be also.

---

[8] **formidable**—difficult.

QUESTIONS TO CONSIDER

1. In what ways does Shethar say the ambulance workers were like the guards at the concentration camp?

2. What is Shethar saying about the little difference between hurting people to help them and hurting people to kill them? What's his point?

3. How do you think he feels about Adolf Eichmann?

4. What do you think people must do to assure that there is never another Holocaust?

War Ends

The Tide Turns on D-Day On June 6, 1944, the invasion of Normandy began the first major step toward ending the war in Europe. It was one of the greatest military battles ever fought. It took more than two years to plan and was a massive effort at coordinating air, ground, and naval assaults on the enemy.

▲
Liberation of Dachau These photos show the prisoners at Dachau, who were liberated by the U.S. Seventh Army on April 30, 1945.

◀ **Liberation** In Europe, the end of the war meant the liberation of thousands of Jews held in German concentration camps.

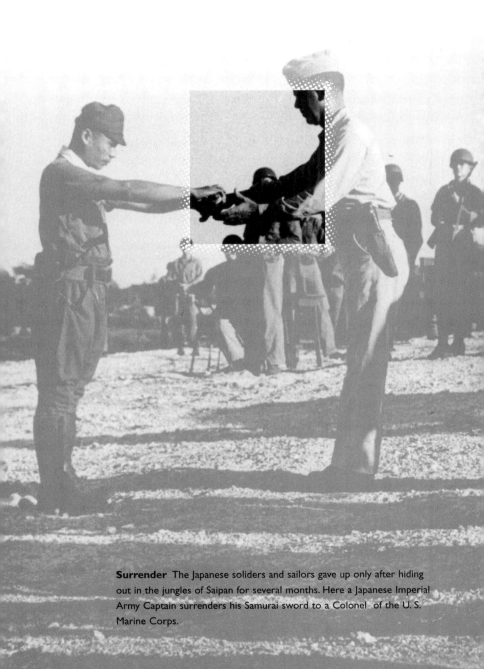

Surrender The Japanese soliders and sailors gave up only after hiding out in the jungles of Saipan for several months. Here a Japanese Imperial Army Captain surrenders his Samurai sword to a Colonel of the U. S. Marine Corps.

Chronology of the War

1918
World War I ends. The Treaty of Versailles punishes Germany.

1922
Benito Mussolini establishes a Fascist Dictatorship in Italy.

1931
Japan invades Manchuria.

1932
Hitler becomes chancellor of Germany.

1933
Germany passes its first law denying rights to Jews.

1936
Italy and Germany sign the Axis pact. Hitler occupies the Rhineland.

1937
Japan begins war against China. Japan joins the Axis.

1938
Hitler takes Austria and the Sudetenland and moves into Czechoslovakia.
November: *Kristallnacht* begins the Holocaust.

1939
August: Stalin and Hitler sign the Nazi-Soviet Non-Aggression Pact. Roosevelt and Churchill issue the Atlantic Charter.

September:
The Germans wage *blitzkrieg* in Poland.

November: The Soviet Union declares war on Finland. Great Britain and France declare war on Germany.

1940
April-May: Hitler attacks Norway, Denmark, France, Belgium, and Holland. Holland surrenders. The British and French armies are rescued at Dunkirk.

June: Italy declares war on France and Britain. Germany overruns France and sets up a puppet government at Vichy. The United States, still neutral, begins its first peacetime draft in history. German submarines begin the Battle of the Atlantic to cut off food and supplies to Britain.

August: Germany begins air raids on Britain.

1941
March: U.S. Congress passes the Lend-Lease Act.

April: German General Erwin Rommel and the Afrika Korps help the Italian forces repel the British from Lybia. Japan signs a neutrality treaty with the U.S.S.R.

June: The German attack on the Soviet Union begins. By **September,** they have reached Leningrad and by **December** they are within five miles of Moscow. Japan attacks the U.S. Pacific Fleet at its base in Pearl Harbor, Hawaii, and the United States enters the war.

1942

January: Twenty-six nations sign the United Nations Declaration. The Allies are formed. By **May**, Japan controls a huge area from deep in China, to most of Southeast Asia, the western Pacific, Burma, Malaya, the East Indies, the Philippines, and all the large islands north of the equator.

June: U.S. Admiral Nimitz defeats Japanese Admiral Yamamoto in the Battle of Midway. The U.S. joins the war in North Africa.

July: The five-month battle for Stalingrad begins.

August: In the Pacific, U.S. Marines land on Guadalcanal and begin the first of six battles that will take them to November. In North Africa, General Bernard Law Montgomery and General Dwight David Eisenhower battle Rommel.

1943

January: The Germans surrender at Stalingrad.

March: Japanese forces score many victories. Saying, "I shall return," U.S. General Douglas MacArthur leaves the Philippine peninsula of Bataan. In North Africa, Rommel begins a drive to the Lybian-Egyptian border.

May–June: U.S. troops in the Pacific retake Attu. In Europe, Germans provide evidence linking the U.S.S.R. to 11,000 Polish officers found in mass graves in the Katyn Forest near Smolensk.

July: Mussolini is stripped of power.

August: Allied troops under Admiral William Halsey move through the Solomon Islands.

September: Italy signs an armistice with the Allies. In the Pacific, MacArthur drives the Japanese back along the east coast of New Guinea.

November: Halsey's forces take a large beachhead on Bougainville. U.S. Marines wage war in the Gilbert Islands.

1944

January: After 27 months of siege, the Soviet forces rescue Leningrad. The Allies retake the Marshall Islands.

February–May: Allied forces make more gains in the Pacific. The last German forces are driven out of Russia.

June: The U.S. defeats the world's two largest battleships, *Yamato* and *Musashi* in the Battle of the Philippine Sea. In Europe, D-Day (June 6) brings the Allied cross-channel invasion to the beaches of Normandy.

July: An assassination attempt on Hitler fails. Rommel commits suicide. The Polish underground initiates the Warsaw uprising against the Germans. Stalin refuses to help because they are anti-Communist.

August: Paris is liberated. Allied forces leave Italy to join the battle for southern France. The Soviets move toward the Black Sea. Romania seeks an armistice from them. In the Pacific, the Allies have Saipan, Tinian, and Guam. They agree not to invade Japan until Germany is defeated and ground troops are available.

September: U.S. patrols cross the German border. In the Pacific, Allied operations in the Carolines and Philippines proceed.

October: The Japanese navy fights its last battle at Leyte Gulf in the Philippines. In Poland, the Germans quash the Warsaw uprising. Soviet troops take Belgrade, Yugoslavia, and set up a Communist government under Marshall Tito.

December: German armies surprise the Americans in the Battle of the Bulge. It takes the Allies until January 16 to restore their front.

1945

January: The Japanese begin kamikaze bombing.

February: U.S. Marines attack Iwo Jima. Stalin, Roosevelt, and Churchill meet at Yalta, and Stalin agrees to enter the war against Japan.

March: Allied armies cross the Rhine.

April: The battle for Okinawa begins. Roosevelt dies, and Truman becomes U.S. president. Allied forces close in on Berlin. Hitler commits suicide.

May: German surrender is signed. May 8 is declared VE Day, for Victory Europe.

June: Allied forces win the battle for Okinawa.

July: The U.S. explodes the first atomic bomb in a test at Alamogordo, New Mexico.

August: The U.S. drops atomic bombs on Hiroshima and Nagasaki. Japan announces surrender on August 14.

September: Japanese surrender is signed in Tokyo Bay aboard the *Missouri*.

ACKNOWLEDGEMENTS

10 Shirer, William. From *Berlin Diary: The Journal of a Foreign Correspondent, 1934-1941* by William Shirer. Reprinted with permission from The William L. Shirer Literary Trust.

15 Nowak, Jan. From *Courier from Warsaw* by Jan Nowak, (c) 1982. Reprinted by permission of the author.

31 Rosenberg, Maxine. "Rose-Silverberg-Skier", from *Hiding to Survive: Stories of Jewish Children Rescued from the Holocaust*. Copyright (c) 1994 by Maxine B. Rosenberg. Reprinted by permission of Clarion Books/ Houghton Mifflin Company. All rights reserved.

51 Babington-Smith, Constance. From *Air Spy: The Story of Photo Intelligence in World War II* by Constance Babington-Smith. Copyright © 1957.

58 Reed, Henry. From *Lessons of the War* by Henry Reed. Reproduced with permission of Curtis Brown Ltd, London, on behalf of the Estate of Henry Reed. Copyright the Estate of Henry Reed.

64 St. Vincent Millay, Edna. "I Forgot for a Moment" by Edna St. Vincent Millay. From *Make Bright the Arrows,* Harper & Brothers. Copyright (c) 1940, 1968 by Edna St. Vincent Millay and Norma Millay Ellis. All rights reserved. Reprinted by permission of Elizabeth Barnett, literary executor.

66 Jarrell, Randall. "Second Air Force" by Randall Jarrell. Copyright (c) 1969 and copyright renewed (c) 1997 by Mary von S. Jarrell. Reprinted by permission of Farrar, Straus & Giroux, Inc.

70 Atlantic Charter. *The Atlantic Charter,* August, 1941.

73 Hoffman, William. From *The Battle for Stalingrad* by Vasili Chuikov, Published by Grafton Books, a division of HarperCollins Publishers Ltd.

82 Nichols, David. From *Ernie's War* by David Nichols. Copyright (c) 1986 by David Nichols. Reprinted by permission of Random House, Inc.

93-100 Mauldin, Bill. Reprinted by permission of Bill Mauldin and the Watkins/Loomis Agency.

101 Vining, Donald. From *American Diaries of World War II,* edited by Donald Vining. Copyright 1982 by Donald Vining. Reprinted with permission of the Estate of Donald Vining.

115 Vining, Donald. From *American Diaries of World War II,* edited by Donald Vining. Copyright 1982 by Donald Vining. Reprinted with permission of the Estate of Donald Vining.

128 Travers, Paul Joseph. From *Eyewitness to Infamy: An Oral History of Pearl Harbor* by Paul Joseph Travers. Copyright © 1991 by Paul Joseph Travers. Reprinted by permission of the author.

141 Roosevelt, Franklin D. *Address to Congress,* December 7, 1941 by Franklin D. Roosevelt.

144 Lidz, Richard. From *Many Kinds of Courage: An Oral History of World War II* by Richard Lidz. Copyright © 1980 by Richard Lidz.

155 Hafford, William E. "The Navajo Code Talkers" by William E. Hafford from *Arizona Highways,* February 1989, vol. 65, no. 2, pp. 36-45.

164 Fahey, James. Excerpt from *Pacific War Diary* by James Fahey. © 1963 by James J. Fahey.

173 Redding, J. Saunders. "A Negro Looks at this War" by J. Redding Saunders. From *American Mercury 55,* November 1942.

188 Trevor-Roper, H.R. *From The Last Days of Hitler* by H.R. Trevor-Roper. Copyright 1947 by H.R. Trevor-Roper.

198 Trumball, Robert. From *Nine who survived Hiroshima and Nagasaki* by Robert Trumball. Copyright © 1957 by Robert Trumball.

208 Shethar, Norman. From speech by Norman Shethar at AFS Conference, October 3, 1993.

Photo research: Diane Hamilton

Index